In Every Season

In Every Season

God's Faithfulness in the Lives of Ordinary Women

Bethany Mae Armstrong

ISBN: 1548091146
ISBN 13: 9781548091149

Dedication

I get my spunkiness from you. My perseverance too.
You were strong and patient and beautiful.
You put wind beneath my wings and taught me how to fly.

I love you, Mama.

Acknowledgements

Claire- Thank you for all the belly laughs and kitchen dances and for believing that I could do this. You will forever be my magnolia.

Liz- You are wise beyond your years; I am thankful that you keep me grounded and that you always know what I need. I will never look at a dragonfly the same way again.

Jack- The most humble person I know; thank you for asking me to dance.

Lydia- Thank you for being my number one cheerleader in every thing I tackle, for the incessant prayers on my behalf, and for meeting me at the moon. I write because of you.

Dixie- I am thankful for the countless hours we have spent discussing our life's journey. I'll be your "straight man" any day.

Allison- Thank you for loving me and mine in every way. You are a gift to me.

Grace– Your generosity and thoughtfulness have been such an encouragement to me. Thank you for using your gifts to bless me so.

Jenna– Thank you for being there at the turns in my life when I needed you most.

Eden– The happiest person I know. Thank you for sharing joy and being a source of positive influence in my life.

S.A.S., HomeBase Girls and Ele-Gals– I can't believe we get to do this life together. Here's to living with the veil off!

Preface

"Give praise to the Lord, proclaim his name; make known among the nations what he has done. Sing to him, sing praise to him; tell of all his wonderful acts. Glory in his holy name; let the hearts of those who seek the Lord rejoice. Look to the Lord and his strength; seek his face always."

1 CHRONICLES 16:8-11

It was in July of 2010 while sitting in a food court in Atlanta's Hartsfield Jackson International Airport that I knew. I knew that I was to share my story. It would not only be my story, but the story of several girlfriends as well. Our stories are no more special than many of yours, but how God was faithful over and over in our lives is a story worth telling.

Four years passed, and I would write in random spare time when something inspired me, but nowhere near answering the call that God laid on my heart. I was busy managing my family's local breakfast and lunch restaurant, and with this came great responsibility. I found myself awake at night worrying about it, getting messages in the wee hours from someone calling in sick, receiving phone calls when I was off or out of town, and being burdened about it because I treated it like it was my own. My head was too clouded to think straight, let alone write, despite repeated nudges from the Holy Spirit to "work on the book". I struggled and toyed with the idea of leaving my job in order to focus on writing, but the idea would be quickly doused with inner thoughts of, "Am I crazy? We can't do that! How will we go from two incomes to one? That seems so irresponsible."

It got to the point where I was praying for God to show me if my two-year stint there was over. He said it was. I wavered and wondered if I heard Him correctly. I prayed for Him to show me if I missed the mark. I remember saying, "Lord, I need you to really let me hear you. I need a billboard-sized answer instead of a gentle whisper, ok, God?" For two months I had my spiritual radar up anticipating His answer. And, I got it. I was sitting on my sofa one Sunday morning listening to Charles Stanley while waiting for my husband to get dressed for church, and I heard the following:

"Be obedient. To disobey is a devastating act of rebellion. God knows what is on the other side of your obedience. You don't. But, you can trust him. Take the next step…without all the answers. If you wait to see your way clear, you will never enjoy the best of God's blessings. This equals faith. Use the skills and talents to do what you are supposed to do. Remember how God has been faithful in your life; you have a biography. You can't operate on fear. If God tells you to do something, He will work it out because that's who God is."

Tears rolled down my cheeks, and I knew what I had to do. Soon thereafter, with my husband's full support and my extended family's blessing, I surrendered to the Lord and made myself available to write full time.

God was so good to answer my prayer and to make clear what He wanted me to do. It sure didn't make sense from the world's perspective or even my own mind, but I let the Spirit lead me into obedience. Two things immediately happened. First, the air conditioning unit in our home completely died and had to be replaced to the tune of $5,800, followed by a $1,300 car repair that same week. *Gulp*. Second, I landed on some powerful Scripture in 1 Chronicles as I was studying the life of David. This is David talking to his son, Solomon, who was soon to be the next king, but it was also God talking to Bethany throughout these two chapters:

22:11-16 "Now my son (Bethany), the Lord be with you, and may you have success and build the house (write the book) of the Lord your God, as he said you would. I have provided you with all the necessary supplies and labor. May the Lord give you discretion and understanding. Be strong and courageous. Do not be afraid or discouraged. Now begin the work and the Lord be with you." 28:10b "Be strong and do the work."

I walked in a spiritual stupor for days as I was blown away at the Lord's timing, encouragement, and validation. I was taking a leap of faith and decided I was going to land on His promises, and He would be faithful, just as He always had.

Part 1

In the Beginning

Tumbleweed

"Remember not the sins of my youth and my rebellious ways; according to your love remember me, for you are good, O Lord."

PSALM 25:7

Growing up, I was the oldest of four children and the only girl. I could hang with the best of them- my three brothers and all of their friends as well. I had my own BB gun, built forts, and coveted the neighbor's dirt bike. I was also a ballerina, cheerleader, and horse lover. One year my granddaddy, Roy, gave me two horseback riding lessons for Christmas. When he saw how much I loved it, he kept taking me. Every Saturday, for two years. Our routine after the lessons consisted of going to McDonalds for Big Macs and hurrying to eat them before we got to the Dairy Queen where we ordered our standard butterscotch-dipped cones. He spoiled me, and I loved him. He was a gentle giant who modeled patience, devotion and quiet strength.

My Granny was spunky, determined and generous. She taught me how to identify many species of birds, how to make milk gravy from scratch, and how to create sugar Easter eggs, which we donated to the local children's hospital where she worked as a secretary. She was proud as punch when I volunteered there as a candy striper.

Granny was proud of me, but I was the apple of my granddaddy's eye. I used to sit in his lap to drive the car down his long driveway. I progressed to sitting on a pillow and ventured onto the back roads, and before long, at the whopping age of *twelve*, I was driving on the highway! It was our little secret, or so we thought. Granny and Mama found out and showed great disapproval and concern. We didn't let it bother us too much; we were just careful not to talk about it around them.

It is easy to see why I spent every possible moment at my grandparent's house a few miles away. My daddy was busy working all the time providing for his family, though I subconsciously craved his approval and validation for many years. My mama was simply surviving as she raised four kids single-handedly. I decided early on that it was my job to be a good girl. I saw how she struggled with three rowdy boys, some of who were always in trouble and causing her grief. I couldn't do much, but I could lay low and not add any stress to the chaos. This deeply rooted trait of desiring to be good would prove valuable later in my walk as a Christian.

We did not attend church as a family, but we were enrolled in a private Christian school. Maybe my parents felt that in doing so, the spiritual base was covered. We didn't talk about God or pray or have a Bible anywhere handy. However, it wasn't uncommon for my granddaddy to drop me off at church. On one such occasion, at the age of seven, I decided to walk down to the altar and accept Jesus as my Savior because… it was the thing to do. I was soon baptized and, that was it. I didn't feel any different and nothing about my life changed.

I grew into my teenage years and outgrew my grandparents. A family move 40 miles away put distance between us, but so did getting a job at the age of 15, which consumed my evenings and weekends. I was a wayward teenager -wayward in the sense that I was lonely and empty and had no direction. I was a good girl, stayed out of trouble, went to school and went to work.

Being plucked from my private school and planted into a public school classroom my junior year was a tough transition for me. Everybody knew everybody. I was there for only two years, which wasn't enough time to establish deep-rooted friendships. I graduated with a class of 200, but felt alone. I decided to fill that void by going to the graduation of my "friends" at the private school. Out of a graduating class of 25, no one paid much attention to me. It seems I didn't belong there either.

Then, the wind blew this tumbleweed into the arms of someone who noticed me, spoke words of affirmation to me, and encouraged me to better myself. I enrolled in college, and I married him.

Part 2

For Better or For Worse

Growing Pains

⁓

*"By the grace God has given me, I laid a foundation
as an expert builder, and someone else is building on
it. But each one should be careful how he builds."*

1 Corinthians 3:10

Marriage agreed with me. College did not. In high school I was
an average B-C student. In my parents' eyes this was great
because they were comparing my grades to some of my brothers', which
often consisted of D's and F's. College was a struggle, and having no
idea what I wanted to do with my life only complicated the matter.

I ended up with a bachelor's degree in psychology with thoughts of
becoming a marriage counselor, only to find out that doing so required
a master's degree in counseling which had to be obtained from a college
out of town. This wasn't very feasible being a newlywed and an expect-
ant mother. My husband had dreams of owning his own business, so
we took the plunge and opened a jewelry store in our small hometown.

I ran it during the day, and he would come in from his job as a teacher in the afternoons to check on things and close up. He wanted to be there more, and I wanted to be there less. I went back to college and obtained my master's degree in teaching, and we switched jobs. He ran the business, and I taught middle school and poured my extra energy into raising our daughter. We were happy and thriving despite constant financial pressure. This pressure brought with it both criticism and fear on my part. I struggled with submitting to my husband, specifically with regards to finances, because I didn't agree with decisions that were being made which were affecting us so negatively.

We were in church every Wednesday and Sunday, mainly because it was the thing to do. He was also on staff. Though I sang hymn after hymn, it didn't go down past my vocal chords; it never entered my heart. I taught fifth grade Sunday school and directed Vacation Bible School for many years. I found this easy to do because I had the head knowledge to do it. As a couple we didn't grow spiritually, and it seems our attempts to do so ended up being all about theology and never about the relationship with Christ that I was hearing so much about. I deeply craved family devotions and wanted to be a couple that prayed together. Mealtime blessings were as close as we got.

Broken Eggs

"The thief comes only to kill and steal and destroy...."

JOHN 10:10

My second year of teaching was coming to a close when we discovered that our family would be growing. Claire was getting a little sister! I was enjoying the summer break and filled my time with pushed-aside-projects, lots of reading, and swimming with my daughter every day.

It wasn't unusual for me to drop by the store to visit my husband to take him lunch or just to say hello. On one such occasion something didn't seem quite kosher. I walked into a way-too-friendly atmosphere, and a red flag went up in my mind. It was a big flag. He and his female employee had the countenance that things were not on the "up and up". I questioned him, and it was explained away, and then the mind games started up inside me. Later that evening I decided to go check things out at the business after my husband closed and went home. I let myself in with a key that I still had on my key ring. Lying on the desk was a sealed letter. To him. From her. I opened it. My heart racing. My stomach at my feet. My hands shaking.

I got home and showed him the letter and interrogated him. He dismissed it as "infatuation". I was not buying it.

A week later I went back to the store after hours and let myself in again. This time, she had gotten a little smarter. His briefcase, which was never locked, was. I knew something was being concealed inside it. I didn't know the combination so I busted it open. And there it was. Another letter. I wasn't prepared for its contents. It was more than infatuation on both parts, and it discussed somewhere they had been, etc. I was devastated. I had put all of my eggs in his basket. I would never be the same. And, I was carrying his second child.

This time I went home and demanded that he fire her. He said she had not done anything wrong and that it was all him. He expressed that he was sorry and that he understood how upset I was. He wouldn't agree to fire her, so I did. I called her and told her I found the letter and that I didn't want her there anymore; I told her to turn her keys in the next day and leave.

Well, I paid for that. He would not talk to me, acknowledge me, or communicate in any way except to say that I crossed the line, and that she didn't do anything wrong. He basically told me that if I wanted things to be right between us I had to agree for her to come back, but he would move her down a few doors to run his tanning bed business.

He kept reassuring me that he loved me and that I had nothing to worry about. It was not an overnight decision, but I had to give in. I was due to deliver our second child in just a few months.

This employee relationship was a major source of contention between us, and I was not happy about her still being around. I made sure he knew it and brought her up often. He would reassure me that I didn't have anything to worry about and that he loved me. Trying to keep a business afloat and handling our increasing debt appeared to be more of a priority to him.

It didn't help matters that a few days after our second daughter was born, I took her to church to support him as he led the choir Christmas cantata. I walked in the sanctuary and there *she* was, sitting with her husband on the second pew. The pew I always occupied.

I was right about one thing. I would never be the same.

Once Was Lost, But Now Am Found

"*But now this is what the Lord says- he who created you, O Jacob, he who formed you, O Israel: "Fear not, for I have redeemed you; I have summoned you by name; you are mine. When you pass through the waters, I will be with you; and when you pass through the rivers, they will not sweep over you.*"

ISAIAH 43:1-2

In the most desperate time of my life I had no one to go to. I couldn't. We were very private about our personal lives so counseling was not an option. I had little free time to invest in friendships so I had no one I could trust with such life-altering circumstances. I was in a dark and lonely place.

But, in the darkness of that pit, there was a Light. His name was Jesus. *He* would not hurt me. *He* would not betray me. *He* was my best friend. My heart and His heart connected in a way that was indescribable, and I decided to pursue Him with reckless abandon. This meant forgiving my remorseful husband. This meant honoring my wedding vows. This meant moving forward and taking my family with me.

And I did.

I fell in love with Jesus. I nurtured a relationship with Him through prayer, Scripture reading and Bible studies. I worshipped Him big and bold and loud.

I poured my life into my daughters and my students and continued to take care of my husband. I had my eyes and ears open for anything shady and things appeared to be okay. He seemed very remorseful, and it wasn't long before he closed the tanning bed business, and she was gone. We were well into twelve years of marriage by this time and seemed to have weathered a horrific storm.

It took a year, but my marriage was restored to 100% trust. I was in awe that I could trust to that degree after what happened. That's just it. I couldn't, but God could. I was so grateful to Him for restoring my marriage and giving us a second chance. My relationship with Christ flourished, and I made it public by rededicating my life to Him one Sunday morning.

The pressure of finances was still bearing down on us, and I continued to struggle with business decisions that were being made because they had an effect on all of our personal finances. This was a constant trickle of discord as I buffered bill collectors calling our home and relayed that info to him the minute he walked in the door. Despite fear and criticism ever present in our relationship on both sides, we tried to hang in there and push through.

We decided to take a road trip to New York City, just the two of us. We enjoyed the sites in several states on the drive up and finally made it to the big city. Late one evening we received a phone call that the burglar alarm was going off at the jewelry store. This meant someone needed to meet the police, check things out, and reset the alarm. Who did he call? *Her.* I was mortified. Why her? He could have called someone else. "There was no one else." I went into total shut down mode. I don't know how we finished that vacation or how we made the long drive home. It was all a blur, except when we pulled up to my parent's home and my daughters catapulted into my arms with hugs and kisses and "I miss yous." I would push through this major set back. For them.

And I did.

Their arms weren't the only ones I landed in. I ran to Jesus, and He met me in my brokenness and angst. My husband reassured me that I didn't have anything to worry about. He told me he loved me, and only me. This kept me afloat, along with focusing on my daughters and starting a new school year. This school year would take more than my normal amount of focus and energy as I was moving to a new school in a new county.

And that is where I met Dixie.

Big Hair and Ruby Red Lips

*"Do not conform to the pattern of this world, but
be transformed by the renewing of your mind. Then
you will be able to test and approve what God's
will is—his good, pleasing and perfect will."*

ROMANS 12:2-3

I found Dixie sitting on top of a desk in the teacher workroom balling her eyes out. I don't remember why she was crying, but we connected immediately, and from there we were inseparable. She was new, and so was I. We taught the same subject in the same grade level, which enabled us to come up with creative ways to teach our students. We had them collecting dryer lint and snack boxes, performing skits, and writing pen pals. The two of us dressed as germs, mimes, and Fred and Barney. We taught "out of the box" to engage our students and led the school in various pep rallies with themes such as the Blues Brothers, "Penny Pencil and Sammy Scantron", and The Streak. (Oh my, that is one I wish to forget). Dixie sure had a way of talking me into things. We were a team, she, the funny guy, and I, the straight man.

This new friend was larger than life, and everything she did, she did big. She cried big, laughed big and tackled every task with 110% gusto. We brainstormed over lesson plans, and our creative juices flowed.

Dixie was the person who made music come alive for me, Christian music to be exact. She loved the Lord and sang of His power and majesty. I was hooked. I started buying cds and worshipping in my car, my classroom, and my home. She sang in church, and I was there to listen and support her. Our youngest daughters were the same age so our friendship naturally and easily grew beyond the classroom.

She was married and raising two stepchildren in addition to her youngest daughter. One evening she called me in hysterics with fear that her husband was being unfaithful. My emotions started whirling with an "I know how you feel" syndrome, and I comforted her the best I could. It wasn't long before she was moving into an apartment and getting divorced.

Dixie attached herself to my hip while trying to find her new normal, and that was fine by me. We would pile our daughters into the car and head to concerts, Six Flags or the beach. She and her daughter would accompany my family to church, which usually included Sunday lunch. She was quickly becoming the best friend I never had.

Our passion for music grew, and Dixie loved singing solos in church. We felt led to pursue this further and started a ministry traveling to area churches where she sang and gave her testimony. Our ministry's business card, complete with butterfly logo read, "Dixie- Soloist, Bethany- Everything Else". I felt like her manager and actually carried out that role by scheduling events, organizing music and lip-syncing when she forgot the lyrics. We were just beginners, but our hearts were in it big. Our first promoted concert looked more like a séance than a church worship service as we draped black cloth all over the altar and banisters, and lined them with every candle we could gather from home. *Cringe.* Some things we wish to forget.

Our daughters were included in the ministry and would travel with us dressed in matching outfits and signing words on stage as Dixie sang. We were booking concerts on a regular basis as word of mouth traveled fast.

One of the church members had a son who sang and played guitar. She suggested we have him create the music for a few songs that Dixie and I had written. We were on our way to stardom with recording plans in our future!

Well, it was love at first sight. Dale and Dixie hit it off and started dating and eventually married. The pressure from my husband for me to be at home more and to keep my priorities in order made it easy for me to step back and let Dale take my place in our singing ministry. They performed together and made such a great team, eventually recording a CD or two.

Life was rocking along for both Dixie and me, and our friendship was taking on a "new normal". In less than a year after marrying Dale, Dixie was diagnosed with breast cancer. Aggressive surgery was suggested, followed by chemotherapy, radiation and reconstructive surgery. It was a very serious time, but anything involving Dixie takes on a different feel. She laughed about me accidentally putting her medication in the freezer instead of the refrigerator after we brought her home from the hospital. One day we went shopping to buy her a dress for an upcoming event. I was helping her in the dressing room trying carefully not to disturb her many drain lines, to which she affectionately referred to as her "pocketbooks". Her sense of humor amazed me.

Dixie's determined drive and personality to beat cancer prevailed. To everyone's astonishment, she rarely missed a day of teaching during her long period of recovery and treatments. This victory over cancer only added to her testimony as she gave God glory yet again.

Dixie and I both ended up transferring to different schools and focused on raising our daughters and loving our husbands. We stayed in touch, but didn't see each other on a regular basis. Just over four years passed, and she was handed the bombshell news that her cancer had returned.

True to form, she fought it again with everything in her and attributed her drive to having a daughter who needed her and to the Lord who was counting on her.

Today, she is cancer free and recalls how God has been faithful in her life's journey...

God is always pursuing me to Himself to answer His call. He has reminded me that I belong to Him and that He has a God-ordained purpose for my life. He has provided me the soothing balm of praise and music that awakens me to the laughter in all of life's circumstances.

He has been faithful in giving me the gift of a child. He has provided wisdom and strength as I've grown older to carry me to a place of hope in Him in every valley and on every mountaintop of my life. He has shown me through my husband and daughter and friends what God's love is.

After my divorce, God was faithful in drawing me to Him and to remind me that in Him I was complete even though I felt incomplete, useless, like used goods. He reminded me that I was His and that He created me and has an ordained purpose for my life. He showed me that when I lean on Him and believe in Him, He sees His Son; He sees me whole and complete and worthy.

God's faithfulness in my battle with cancer showed me that He was a restorer. He was a healer...I had been broken emotionally, relationally, financially, but having cancer was the first time that I was physically broken, and I strongly identified with Christ's physical suffering on the cross. In my second bout with cancer He showed me I needed to press on and that evil had no power over me because "greater was He that was in me than he that was in the world," I John 4:4. God was faithful to remind me to live...."Don't die 'til you're dead" was my motto derived from Psalm 118:17, "I shall not die but live and declare the works of the Lord of which I am one." A friend once said to me, "Do you want your daughter to remember you dying or remember you living?" And my answer was, to remember me living. And that has been my answer ever since.

God is faithful to always remind me to answer the call that He has on my life which is to spread the good news of the gospel through Jesus Christ with as much passion, compassion and laughter as possible.

~ Dixie

Rocking Along

~

"My heart says of you, 'Seek his face!'
Your face, Lord, I will seek."

PSALM 27:8

My sweet little family thrived on eating dinner together every night, church activities, and campaigns. Political involvement was important to my husband and so we all supported him in this endeavor. I didn't like politics, but I loved him so I was willing to help. I made countless phone calls to constituents during elections and dressed as Betsy Ross in campaign parades. Claire and Liz could be found sealing envelopes and waving campaign signs. We embraced the whole idea and believed in him through several political races despite the public ever voting him into office.

I had a desire to seek the Lord and to grow spiritually but didn't know how to go about it. Picking up the Bible and reading it felt like the right thing to do, but I wasn't getting very far in broadening my spiritual horizons. Then came Beth Moore. She made the Word come alive, and I began to understand Scripture on such a deeper level. This also started the process of peeling some of the layers of who I was, and some of it wasn't pretty. I had a deep issue of comparing myself to others and living behind a veil. I didn't want others to see my flaws. Envy and jealousy could also be found in my mixed bag of sins.

As previously mentioned, my husband and I never verbalized to anyone about our struggles, either as a couple or individually. I was instructed not to share about things that were personal. This made taking the veil off rather difficult. However, the more I studied, I found myself slowly gravitating to what the Lord was instructing me to do through His Word…

Encourage others. To do so one must be real. You can't pretend you are perfect or that your life is all a bed of roses.

"Now the Lord is the Spirit, and where the Spirit of the Lord is, there is freedom. And we all, who with unveiled faces contemplate the Lord's glory, are being transformed into his image with ever-increasing glory, which comes from the Lord, who is the Spirit." II CORINTHIANS *3:17-18*

I slowly began to trust friends with the real me and shared from my heart. Claiming and living the above verse was a turning point in my walk with Christ.

My Alli

"*I will lead the blind by ways they have not
known, along unfamiliar paths I will guide them;
I will turn the darkness into light before them
and make the rough places smooth. These are the
things I will do; I will not forsake them.*"

ISAIAH 42:16

Allison is my feel-like-we've-never-been-apart girlfriend to the core. We had a God-ordained introduction on the sidewalk of Brentwood Elementary School where her son and my youngest daughter were in the same Pre-K class, and her daughter and my oldest daughter were in the same fourth grade class. It was "friends at first sight," and it was meant to be.

A nurse by profession, Allison has the most caring spirit. She is bright and humorous and genuine. She can answer just about any medical question with great accuracy. If you have nice, plump veins in your arms, she will notice. She is liable to start rubbing them while drooling and talking about how fat and juicy they are for sticking.

She is a class act and should be on a theatre stage somewhere. We were at dinner celebrating the big 50th birthday of several friends a few years back. Out of the bathroom and up to our table walks this old lady with a cane and big pocket book, white hair and spectacles, knee-highs rolled to just above the ankles, low hanging breasts and an exaggerated rear end. It was Allison. She had changed in the bathroom. In the center of the restaurant she was addressing the birthday girls with "I remember whens" and telling "over the hill" jokes. The whole place was in stitches.

I have seen her show up at the bedside of many hospital patients, who were complete strangers but were friends or family of people that she cared about. She would sing. She would pray. She would evaluate and she would encourage. Everyone always feels better after being in Allison's presence.

Allison is real. As real as you get. She is honest, transparent and always attentive and willing to help. She pours herself into the people close to her.

Here is her story…

Early in our friendship, Bethany and I were at a local restaurant one day having lunch when, during the course of conversation, I felt led to tell her the truth of who I really was. She had alluded to the fact that things were not right in her marriage. She didn't come right out and say it, but I got the impression that her husband had been unfaithful. She was very protective of him and wasn't going to tarnish his reputation in any way. Observing how she treated him was very eye opening to me.

Despite hurt and disappointment she still did her best to remain faithful to him and his reputation. I was so afraid to tell her everything because I thought it would surely bring about judgment and an end to our newfound friendship. To tell someone who had been cheated on that I was a cheater, Mmm, scary stuff. But I shared my story and surprisingly, amazingly, incredibly...all I got was grace! From that day to this, and everything that's happened in between, she never waivered in her grace. That was a picture of Jesus. I had never sensed in a real way that Jesus had that much grace for me; I had never seen that in anyone before. I had lived my life with mistrust and suspicion because too many people- my parents, siblings, friends, and coworkers had disappointed me and used my shortcomings against me when I was vulnerable.

Another part of my personality has been what I call "touch and go". Think of an airplane that touches down on the tarmac, rolls along and slows down a bit but then takes off again into the wild, blue yonder. With friends, my modus operandi had been to, relationally, go deep for a while, touch to the bone marrow, "be all up in there with ya" and then I would drop off the face of the earth. For months. But Bethany never held that against me. She never got mad or gave up on me as a friend. She always let me be me, and she was there waiting on me when I returned with open arms. She kept on being Jesus. To say that Almighty God gave Bethany as a gift to me is to proclaim the beginning foundation and enduring gift of my healing emotionally and spiritually. A large part of my healing has been because of the Lord gifting her with an unwavering desire to run after Jesus, staying close to His hem and a consistent, non-judging, thoughtful, truth telling personality.

From that point, Bethany was very intentional about "loving me to Jesus" no matter what. Emmaus, HomeBase, Bible Studies, talking parenting, and having sleepovers with our daughters. This was God being faithful to me. In our friendship, the Lord has been faithful through the consistent faithfulness of Bethany through everything... my mom's lengthy illness and death, me being a cheater, my marital turmoil, struggling to be a good mother and my emotionally intense job as a nurse.

Despite all these things, I found myself, once again, going down a road I NEVER imagined going down. I found myself in a romantic relationship with another woman. I met her in preparation for a mission trip to Central America. I was learning to speak Spanish and also saw an opportunity to lead her to the Lord. This woman not only came to the Lord, but she was also reconciled to her family. Over time, and after returning from the mission trip, the friendship morphed into the inappropriate. The odd thing is that in my sin, I began to doubt what Bethany was telling me. She pleaded with me to see that the enemy had orchestrated this and was trying to ruin my family, my reputation and ultimately, my witness. What began as a desire to lead this young woman to faith in Christ ended in sin. I "stole the tithe". I took her for myself. This relationship and my thought processes began a two-year downward spiral away from the Lord. I found myself asking, "Is the devil real or am I actually the one making these choices? Is this something that Satan's setting up, as Bethany said, or was it just me and my unfaithful self?" Once a cheater always a cheater, right? The relationship itself didn't feel evil, but the continued adultery and sex attraction did feel wrong...to the core. I eventually began to consider that maybe my thoughts weren't from Satan, but the circumstances leading up to all this must surely have been set up by the evil one, as he knew I would sabotage myself with my own weaknesses and distrust of the Lord.

About this time, I started going to HomeBase. This is where Bethany and Lydia spoke the truth to me in love. I know it broke their hearts to watch me move away from the Lord. My mind was so deceived that I thought no one really cared.

I finally came to my senses and ended the relationship. Two months later, someone I considered to be a long-time friend, contacted my daughter and told her about this relationship I was in, not knowing I had ended it. My daughter!! He contacted my daughter! She was so disappointed and was completely devastated. Although she was angry, she calmly told me I needed to tell her daddy, or else she would. She said I needed to be honest with him and give him the opportunity to make choices for himself in light of the truth. This time, it was the straw that broke the camel's back of my marriage. I had been living in secrecy, shame and darkness. The fear and realization of my sin becoming public paralyzed me. I saw no end to this shame, no future with my children, friends, neighbors, church or community. Suicide seemed a viable option. Today, I thank God for His protection over me during those dark days.

It has never been second nature for me to see a situation and learn from it based on other people's mistakes. My strongest lessons have come from experience- from doing the wrong thing and getting caught. Or, not getting caught, living in it for a time then eventually trying to extricate myself from the wrong I had committed. Over and over this had been my pattern. I have heard that sin will keep you longer than you wanted to stay, take you further than you wanted to go and cost you more than you wanted to pay. I can attest that this is true.

It has been seven years of trying to return to the Lord. This prodigal wanted to come home to Jesus. Really come home. Come home in a way I never authentically understood before. I have no idea what's ahead, but knowing the faithfulness that He has shown me to this point, there's no telling. There's a whole lot more grace and faithfulness that I never trusted before. But no matter what, He's not changing. That's not to say that in coming back to Him, there won't be pain, hardship and tears (consequences, ya know?). But God keeps dropping Himself in there, some way. His faithfulness to me has been in finding out that what's been in my brain, my thoughts and behaviors, is okay. Not okay from a sin perspective but in the fact that He loves me anyway. He became righteousness FOR ME. I am clean! I am pure! I am HIS!

Looking back, my motive was not evil, but I learned I was trying to fill my void with something other than God. I know now that being ripped open and disemboweled in front of everyone had to happen. I came to understand that I put church, my multiple church activities, work and my children as priority before God. Other idols were my friends, being the life of the party, trying to please people and be significant. All these "things" were a thick mask that acted as a barrier to understanding who God really is! Without really knowing Him, I have no chance of knowing who I am. It is because of my relationship with Him that I understand my significance, that I am the daughter of a Good Father and He calls me His own.

So here's what I know today:

If we can trust God's heart towards us and get past our own shame then God can use anything. Nothing is wasted. Nothing. His grace is bigger than our sin if we turn and trust Him with it. I am finally at a place where I can allow myself to believe in His future grace as well. I know I will fail Him again in some way. I know it. But, He will remain faithful. My seeking Him and His ways, with no idols before Him, strengthens our bond. My obedience doesn't buy me an easy way. My motivation now isn't having the easy way. It's to BE His girl. That's all. My heart's desire is to know He is pleased with me and to run after

Him with my whole life (Hey! That sounds like a girl I know named Bethany!). There is nothing I have done or will do that will keep Him from loving me. I'll never be able to make this up to Him.

As for my children, their forgiveness has come. It is established and true. My daughter's prayers for her mother to be reconciled to God were heard. Bethany and my other girlfriends and also my colleagues have all prayed for me and encouraged my NEW and authentic walk with God.

I have always wanted to walk in real confidence, in faith, as a Godly woman. All this time I thought I wasn't Godly or righteous. I thought I wasn't doing enough, that I wasn't clean enough because of my pleasure-seeking, self-seeking. But I **am** righteous because I am right with God and it's because of Him, not me. There is so much release and rest in that. And so what's happening now? I am growing my confidence and my faith, that I already am righteous, and I have been all this time when I thought I wasn't.

In closing, it is important for me to state that people will go to great depths to feel loved and to fill a void...drugs, alcohol, pornography, food, sexual promiscuity, etc. These things just leave us wanting more of "the thing" which leaves less and less room for God. It also leads to shame, and shame is dangerous. In shame, we end up hiding. We become ineffective. If you are a people-pleaser like I am, this makes it even worse. If you are a perfectionist, it makes you want to cover it up even more.

And that's what I'm working on now at 55. I'm a work in progress. We are all a work in progress. I am my Beloved's and my Beloved is mine.

~ Allison

The Pulpit and the Pew

"Therefore, as God's chosen people, holy and dearly loved, clothe yourselves with compassion, kindness, humility, gentleness and patience. Bear with each other and forgive whatever grievances you may have against one another. Forgive as the Lord forgave you."

COLOSSIANS *3:12-13*

Second pew on the left. First seat. That was my spot. I filled this seat for many years in the ebb and flow of church life. My husband was on staff as music director and stood behind the pulpit Sunday after Sunday, Wednesday after Wednesday leading traditional hymns. He worked closely with the pastor each week to plan the order of service. He was responsible for guest soloists and groups, leading the choir, cantatas, and special music.

This particular seat that I occupied, that of the music minister's wife, was a gateway to the behind-the-scenes of church work. I was privy to information that most church members were never exposed to. The inner workings of the church are political and not very pretty at times. We had ridden the roller coaster of several different pastors filling that role, and for a time, were without such a leader. I had a very strong desire to use my leadership and people skills to help remedy that. Through prayer and the support of my husband, I joined the Pastor Search Committee. To my astonishment, they selected me as head of the committee. I didn't see that coming.

Résumés started pouring in, and the committee proceeded to dig through them. My husband would ask me how things were coming along, and I would give him frequent updates. Then I started receiving his opinions. In our committee meetings, his opinions swirling around in my head did not match that of the committee members'. I realized I had a problem. The direction that the committee wanted to take conflicted with what my husband thought was best for the church. I was stuck. And I was essentially hiring his boss.

We spent countless hours at home churning through the "buts" and "what ifs" and before long were arguing about what should be done. I was the head of the committee, and my job was to work with the committee. There was a definite conflict of interest, and I was right in the middle.

Accusations of false answers given in the pastor search committee interview with a prospective pastor began to surface. It's sad to say there was also some underhanded manipulation within the committee itself, only discovered after the fact. Discovered after the pastor was voted in. Discovered after my husband's new boss was hired. This did not set well with him, and he dug his heels in hard. The Pastor Search Committee rolled over into the Pastor Relations Committee to ensure a smooth transition for the pastor and for the congregation, and I was still head of the committee.

There was even more friction at home due to how things had transpired. My husband resisted the decision the church made to vote this pastor in. My husband wanted what was best for the church, and he didn't feel that this pastor was it. He wouldn't let it go and voiced his opinion at church and at home. I began to resent some of the committee members for manipulating events that brought this pastor in. The ripple effects reached all the way into my home. It was a source of contention between us.

I prayed for God to show me what to do in this precarious situation. I knew I needed to keep my priorities in order and soon resigned from the Pastor Relations Committee. We continued to attend, but my husband chose not to bring his Bible into the sanctuary. He was sending a message, and I was starving. The sermons were dry and somewhat empty. I chose to lead a ladies' Sunday school class and facilitated the Beth Moore study that had made God's Word come alive for me.

As a budding believer I recognized that just because we are Christians does not mean we won't have challenges and suffering. It does not mean that things won't be hard. In my efforts to serve, the enemy saw an opportunity to attack me personally. He caused great confusion in my mind and insecurity in my heart. I had a hard time being real and taking the veil off with these ladies because so much of my growth and testimony was about my husband and our marriage and the situation with the pastor. For so many years I remained silent about personal matters, and I kept a certain amount of distance because I was the wife of a staff member.

Through my submission and obedience, God was faithful. Even though I questioned my ability to lead this class, I found purpose. This is where I received spiritual nutrition. I was learning and growing as a Christian and was challenged to apply what I was studying:

Forgive. Speak the truth in love. Trust God.

His Ways Are Not Our Ways

"See to it that no one misses the grace of God and that no bitter root grows up to cause trouble and defile many."

HEBREWS 12:15

It didn't make sense to me why things turned out the way they did with the Pastor Search Committee. We bathed the process in prayer from the beginning. We had others praying. The results were not how I had imagined them. I wanted a pastor who was on fire for the Lord, who challenged me with the spoken Word, and who had a presence of the Holy Spirit. I craved all of this for myself and for the members of our church.

I was dry. Desert dry. Spiritual guidance in my life was missing, and I felt as if I had been under attack by the enemy for months. I was extremely dissatisfied and depressed. This dissatisfaction moved from church, to my job, and to my marriage. The demands and unreasonable expectations as a teacher wore me down, and my marriage felt completely empty. Over many months, satan (the little "s" intentional) used this dissatisfaction to convince me that I didn't love my husband anymore. I was hanging by a thread.

God worked on my heart and showed me to have peace in Him and not my circumstances. I also had a healthy fear of the consequences of my sin and the effect it had on my daughters. I claimed Psalm 37:4, *"Delight yourself in the Lord and he will give you the desires of your heart."* This encouraged me to pursue God with everything I had, and He would take care of me and what I needed. I also learned from Scripture not to give up...others would be saved if I pressed on.

The idea of my family moving to another church had surfaced from time to time through all of this, and now I chose to keep it in the forefront of conversation with my husband. All the time. I was dissatisfied, and I wanted out. I had given it all I had, and after fifteen years, I was ready to move on. But, Sunday after Sunday we kept going. I was trying to follow my husband's lead, and he wasn't budging. I kept praying and waiting on the Lord. And, I kept studying and learning...There is a purpose in the waiting. There is something to learn. Everything has to fall in line before God moves. He will wait until the burden gets so heavy so that He will get the glory and not us. We are not to hide our burdens because others need to see God working miracles.

My husband knew how miserable I was, and he finally gave me the okay to attend church with Allison. When I visited, I was challenged spiritually. I felt as if I were sitting under a fountain! I was learning. I felt the presence of the Holy Spirit through the music. I was alive! This made going back to my home church even harder.

I began to pray for my family to join this church. I yearned for it, and I joyfully shared my experiences with my husband.

Finally he was ready to leave our church of fifteen years; he started attending Allison's church with me. We completed the new membership class and were presented to the congregation at the end of the service one Sunday. It is no exaggeration to say that I wanted to run up and down in front of that altar waving my purple membership book over my head while praising God. I had been in the desert for SO LONG, and now I was in an oasis. God had answered my prayer, and I wanted everyone to know it! I wanted Him to be glorified.

What did I learn in all of this?

One, man will let us down. We have to love people as Jesus does despite their shortcomings.

Two, relationships change. Every relationship is different today than it was a year ago, five years ago. Our relationship with Christ only gets stronger if we pursue Him.

Three, keep our priorities in order. God does not want us to sacrifice something that He has shown is a major priority in our lives.

Four, we cannot be anyone's Holy Spirit.

And finally, in the waiting, we have to give it all we've got. Try everything we can to make "it" work. Whether it is for a future spouse, a child, a job, a marriage, or church home, honor God in the waiting. When it's time, He will move. It is only then that we will have peace. And His peace is abundant and powerful.

Ebb and Flow

~

*"It is for freedom that Christ has set us free.
Stand firm, then, and do not let yourselves
be burdened again by a yoke of slavery."*

GALATIANS 5:1

At any given moment, one can survey his or her circumstances and observe positive and negative things happening simultaneously. It's not so much about mountain top highs and valley lows, but more like the parallel rails of a train track, good happening right along with bad.

My daughters were happy and thriving and were the bright spots in my days. Bill collectors continued to call. Friendships were growing and deepening. My mama was chronically ill. I was soaking up all that I was experiencing, in addition to serving at my new church home. I found out *she* had been hanging out at the jewelry store. My husband said there was nothing to it, and all the trust that I had worked so hard for, was gone. I told him I wanted to leave him.

I privately sought Godly counsel from my new pastor, and for the first time, I was able to tell someone what I had been going through. Everything. With his guidance I learned that I had to focus only on God and let someone else pray for my girls and my husband. I had to love my husband unconditionally and respect him. I had to do everything to try and make it work; leave no stone unturned. When thoughts came in my mind, I had to take them captive and replace them with God. It was okay to hold my husband accountable. Even though I wanted to pull away and distance myself, I needed to move toward him and let him see me changed.

When I sat down with my husband to talk, he said he was sorry. He said nothing mattered if things weren't right between us. He knew how serious I was and how bad things had become when I told him I wanted to leave. He had been there (divorce) once, and it was not something he wanted to do again.

I prayed for God to help me love this man again and to put that desire back in my heart. I recognized that I had not allowed myself to be happy with him. I had entertained satan's lies that he didn't deserve me, that he wasn't saved, and that we didn't have anything in common, and I fantasized about divorcing him. I knew I had to press in and love him as much as I could. I wanted him to see a change in me, and I prayed for God to remove the scales from his eyes and show him Jesus. I had to stop trying to control things and trust God.

It wasn't long before God laid it on my heart that I needed to take care of the things I had been given. My home. My husband. My children. My job. I was to honor God in all of these areas. I needed to rise above my circumstances every day and honor Him. I needed to take my eyes off of what God was doing and focus on who God was. This was the way I could have joy no matter what I was going through.

It is important to acknowledge that I had fierce mental battles with the enemy. *How can I trust him? Is she still around? Why is he working late? Who is he calling? What if?* I could decide to act on these thoughts and dig stuff up, or I could decide to ask God to take over and to help me overcome my weaknesses. He was always faithful to do so. One day God whispered to me in His still small voice, **"You have to let your husband see the Bethany that I have created you to be. Not the betrayed, untrusting wife that satan wants to create, but the one who has been redeemed by the blood of the Lamb. The one who can trust in Me and turn to Me for strength."**

In the months that followed, God moved. Our new church home was a soothing balm to our hearts and minds. My husband respected the pastor, and we were together in Sunday school for the first time in over ten years. I delighted myself in the Lord and He was giving me the desires of my heart. We were experiencing the presence of the Holy Spirit as we worshipped.

Another election found us waving signs and praying (not together, mind you). He had campaigned for months, and Election Day was drawing near. I had no clue what the outcome would be. My prayer was that he would see God in whatever the results were. I just wanted to honor God and continue living daily to serve and glorify Him. I wanted to lead people to the Lord and to continue nurturing relationships in order to do so.

I could not have imagined the incredible consequences of doing that very thing.

Never Say Never

"Glorify the Lord with me; let us exalt his name together."

PSALM 34:3

In my 15th year of teaching, my principal asked me to consider taking over the gifted education program. I was humbled and honored that she had the confidence in me to do that successfully. My head was swirling with doubt, but the challenge appealed to me. It would mean a big change professionally, and I wasn't sure what to do. I decided to make a list of pros and cons to help me make a decision. Halfway into making this list I realized that by the time I finished, it would be about equal. I put my pencil down and thought, "This list is not going to get me anywhere." I asked God to show me what He wanted me to do, to show me what was best for His kingdom glory. I wanted to be in His will. This proved to be a watershed moment and a pivotal shift in the way I made decisions from this point forward.

I decided to take the new position, and the following fall, I hit the ground running, or rolling you might say. The school was filled to capacity, and I did not have a classroom. I had an office and a cart to push around, and I would use other teachers' classrooms when their students were not present.

This is how I got to know Lydia. She shared her room, and I shared my Jesus. Not "in her face" kind of sharing, in fact I didn't realize what I was doing exactly. It felt like I was on autopilot. We would chat here and there, and then I invited her to the Walk to Emmaus, which is a weekend of spiritual renewal and life changing love of God. She went, and she will tell you she has never been the same. I think she put it something like this, "I was plugged in, but there was no electricity going to my outlet."

We collaborated our efforts teaching gifted 8th grade writing. We started brainstorming and a great project evolved. Our students wrote the first literary magazine for our school. We continued this endeavor for the next four years and perfected the project, so much so that our local school board, County Chamber of Commerce and the Georgia State Department of Education recognized us. We were also asked to present at two statewide educational conferences. We were excited to do this, but scared to death. On one such occasion, I vividly remember us going out to the car to play Nicole C. Mullins' "Gon' Be Free" several times to get our nerves under control.

Not only were we sharing music, a love of nature, chai teas and tennis matches, but we were also sharing in His Word. We started digging in a Bible study, just the two of us, and were amazed at what God was showing us. It was a very big deal to be vulnerable and real with another person. God calls us to take the veil off, but doing so is another thing all together.

The following journal excerpt describes what our time together was like for me:

We strategically pick the day and time and guard it as best we can. As we sink into the burgundy sofa and crack open our study, we gradually shift from this world to His.

His world is full of truth and revelations like two friends turning over rocks to discover gems. The rocks are sometimes too heavy, which requires strength and wisdom from both of us, or taking turns back and forth until we get the job done.

His world is full of forgiveness as we uncover yucky things-things that are shared in complete security and unconditional love.

There are deep revelations that cannot be written down and are barely able to be reiterated. These things are captured in our hearts, then they seep down to our soul, and we are changed from the inside out.

Unimaginable. Indescribable. The God-birthed friendship connection, the confessions considered, the darkness snuffed out by the Light, the truth tucked in tight and hearts overflowing with gratitude and amazement that God could understand us in the deepest part of our souls.

It felt good to have someone to share deeply and spiritually with. I needed someone to hold me accountable and give me reminders along the way. I was desperate for encouragement and so thankful I didn't have to go at it alone. After all, life was tough. I was fighting demons and needed someone to come alongside me and to keep me pointed up.

I wasn't the only one struggling. Lydia and her husband had been divorced for many years but remained in the same house to continue raising their two children. Tempers often flew and opinions rarely aligned. There was a lot of discord and fighting. For several years she pursued another relationship but remained at home and was content. Or so she thought.

I remember exactly where we were when we had a conversation about her family and ex-husband. The Lord pressed upon me to say, "You know, God might want you to get back together with your ex-husband. Maybe he wants to restore your marriage."

"Absolutely not," was her response. "Evidently I haven't made myself very clear to you."

I just smiled and chuckled to myself and thought, "Yeah, but God has other plans." And somehow I knew that God was going to do exactly that.

The Lord started to nudge her with the idea of reconciling with her husband. Her husband wanted nothing of God, and she wanted nothing of a restored marriage. She was in love and happy. God wanted more. God wanted total surrender of her life...key word here...TOTAL. She dug her heals in and fought the idea of being back in a relationship with her husband and certainly didn't want to let go of her current relationship. God was not letting up on His pursuit, and His timing was right on time. In our study *Having a Mary Spirit* by Joanna Weaver, we were reading about doing God's will and were prompted with this question: "God, I'll do whatever you want, but please don't ask me to _____."[1] We had to fill in the blank, and Lydia's response was, "end this relationship and go back to my ex-husband."

It was the hardest thing she ever had to do, but she did it. With great angst and pain and suffering, for months and months.

We were coming to the understanding in our studies that God will ask us to do some hard things, and He wants us to obey. This doesn't mean it will be easy, but it means we have to trust him. He wants us to surrender fully to Him. When we do that, God can do His work.

It took time. It took several years as a matter of fact for Lydia's ex-husband to see that God had truly done a transformation in her life. She wasn't just talk, and it took a while for him to be convinced and for him to begin to want what she had. Slowly, very slowly, God began to chip away at the wall he had put up, and his heart began to soften. He began attending church with her and singing in the choir. This, in itself, she called a miracle. God was moving in their relationship and growing them together as a couple.

It is important to mention that it was not super smooth or easy. There were setbacks. There was a broken heart hanging in the balance. There were old habits and patterns to deal with, as well as the enemy not wanting God to be glorified in any of this.

Lydia speaks of His faithfulness and continues her story…

Faithfulness means steadfast, loyal, constant. God has certainly been faithful to me. I spent my whole life searching for something. When I was a little girl I would have a recurring dream. I would be asleep and be reaching out to something, but couldn't quite grasp it. I thought if I could stay asleep a little longer, I could reach it. It was all knowledge and truth. It was not of this world. It was intangible. I had this dream for years. In my waking state I would look for this "something" to fill the void, and focused particularly on Ben. I married him and soon discovered that he was being unfaithful.

Neither one of us were walking with the Lord. My commitment to him doubled as resentment because I would "give in" and stick it out. This tore away at my self-confidence, and I felt like a doormat. I had a temper, and he had words. We used them both destructively. His continued unfaithfulness prompted me to buy a new bed and set it up in another room. When I was putting that bed together, I distinctly heard God call my name. It was a shock. Even though God protected me from myself when I was an impetuous, impulsive youth and young adult, I hadn't had a relationship with Him up to this point in my life. It was a quick awakening that became a gradual pursuit on my part.

Meanwhile, Ben and I divorced and to my surprise, God was faithful in keeping us together in our home. I was sure Ben would leave the minute it was final. We ate dinner together as a family and continued to raise our kids as we "played marriage". Things were still rocky with tempers flaring and words flying, but we stuck it out. I was still looking for that "something" and pursued another relationship and was very happy. This is how life rocked on for a long time.

It would be years later that people started to show Jesus to me in real and natural ways. God was faithful to lead me to a local church to call home and the members there showed me God's incredible love. Bethany introduced me to Walk to Emmaus, and it was there that I was forever changed. I prayed for Christ to be the center of my home, and I accepted that wide open. That weekend I totally surrendered my life to Him.

It didn't happen at all like I envisioned. God started transforming and reshaping many of my relationships. It was not easy. Every time I tried to get closer with God, I experienced what I now know was spiritual warfare. God showed me He wanted to resurrect my marriage. I was met with resistance from my "husband"; in addition to that, my heart ached for the meaningful relationship that God told me I had to give up.

In July of 2011, with our kids by our side, my "husband" and I exchanged wedding vows. In the following years while I waited for Christ to become the center of our home, God blanketed me with His peace, presence and protection. But, I still struggled. My weapon was prayer. Sometimes I would leave the room every two minutes to pray. I found that the Holy Spirit empowered me when I got on my knees.

When I lost my mom, the Lord continued to be faithful. He covered me with sweet peace as I held her hand while she took her last breath. He was steadfast by allowing me to minister to my step-dad in his last days. God showed mercy as I unexpectedly lost a best friend. Lynne told me she was ready to go to her heavenly home, and God was swift to grant her that desire.

I have also experienced God's faithfulness while serving in the Emmaus Community. The Holy Spirit is always present in the testimonies, details, prayers and partnering with others as we come together and watch the pilgrims get exactly what they need.

God is good to give me soul-deep satisfaction and childlike awe of nature. He has blessed Ben and me with a booming kayak business doing what we love and working where we have played for forty years. We have been able to bless and help others simultaneously. He has also made our dream come true as we recently built our retirement home along the edge of the South Edisto River.

You see, God created us with a void so that we would search for Him to fill that void. We often look to fill it with people, drugs, food, work, etc. He is the only answer. God offers us a choice. Sometimes when we choose Him, when we choose total surrender, it brings about some of the hardest things He will ask us to do. When we fill in our blanks, the "God I'll do anything, just please don't ask me to _____" blanks, He honors us. The trials of pain are recycled for gain.

And I wouldn't have it any other way.

~Lydia

It has been twelve years since I walked into that classroom, and today we are still in Bible study. Still digging. Still searching. Still yearning to know Him more. She is my number one cheerleader, the person who knows me best, and my intercessory prayer warrior seeking the Lord on my behalf. She is my partner in crime and partner of accountability. She is the most generous and selfless person I know. I am blessed to call her mine.

I'll Do Anything

"*The cords of death entangled me; the torrents of*
destruction overwhelmed me. The cords of the grave
coiled around me; the snares of death confronted me."

PSALM 18:4-5

In the spring of 2006, I purchased a new vehicle. Lydia and I
would hop in it, open the moon roof, pop in a favorite CD and
cruise and sing and draw close to the Lord. We affectionately referred
to this as "Piloting". That same spring Granny fell and broke her hip. I
spent the majority of her hospital stay by her bedside writing my Teacher
of the Year questionnaire essays. My faculty had selected me to represent
our school at the county level, and it was one of the most humbling, yet
validating highlights of my life.

Though Granny was very independent and lived alone, she definitely needed help after she went home. I was her sole caregiver as Mama
was too sick to take care of her.

One night I was staying at her house and Lydia came by. We were visiting and hanging out and Granny needed help turning in the bed. Lydia jumped right up and had her rolling over in no time. My heart was overwhelmed with gratitude and wonder that she would do that for someone I loved so much.

My calendar was very packed around this time. I was teaching a youth Sunday school class and served as a youth pod leader. Claire was a high school senior making college preparations, which included phone calls, paperwork, college visits, and senior pictures to name a few things. Liz was a cheerleader, in Social dance, tumbling classes and making voice recordings for radio commercials. She did not have a driver's license yet. Granny required assistance with numerous doctors' visits, and so did both of my girls. These things along with teaching and my normal cooking, cleaning, and grocery shopping responsibilities had me spread thin.

I was happy doing all of these things, yet so tormented in my thought life. There didn't have to be any "red flags" for the enemy to get me in a pit of darkness and despair. All he had to do was push my memory buttons. In addition, my husband and I were never without financial burdens and pressure, but I managed to continue my pursuit of Jesus with reckless abandon. What do I mean by reckless abandon? I define it as reckless- adj.: no matter what, don't think, only pursue, don't worry about consequences or what others may think; abandon- verb: leave everything else behind.

I remember having a conversation with my husband one day. I asked him if he thought we connected spiritually. My great desire was to have a spiritual relationship with him where we prayed and sought the Lord together and had family devotions. His analytical answers left me feeling worse after the conversation rather than encouraged. Regardless, good did come out of it because I gave God my marriage. It made me surrender to the Lord even more. I moved from focusing on my marriage less and my personal relationship with God more.

Author Joanna Weaver explains surrender like this: "When we surrender our lives to Jesus Christ, we release the Lord of the process to do His work. For it is in our weakness that Christ is strong. It is in our inadequacy that we find Him more than sufficient. And it is in our willingness to be broken that He brings wholeness, more wholeness and completeness than we ever dreamed possible."[2]

In addition to my marriage, I also surrendered our finances. I decided to submit to my husband's authority with a "whatever he says, goes" mentality, even if I didn't agree. I gave it to God first, for Him to work and bless us despite our mistakes, but I gave it to my husband for the daily walking it out. His business was a sole proprietorship so all of our personal finances were wrapped up with the finances of the business. I couldn't totally submit to my husband and to God while at the same time fuss and complain and stress over money.

Four days later I responded to a knock at my door and found the cable guy standing there. He came to pick up our digital box and proceeded to cut off the 23 stations we were getting. Liz was watching TV at the time. I had to tell my daughters that we didn't have $200 of the $361 that was past due to pay the cable bill, and, that times were tough and this is one of the risks of being in business and to remember it one day when they got married.

Liz said, "What can we do? Let's make a plan so we can get ahead."

Claire added, "You need to help dad make these decisions. It needs a woman's touch. (Out of the mouths of babes?) Instead of watching TV tonight, we can make peanut butter cookies and play Phase 10. And I don't need my $20 allowance this week."

Liz replied, "Me neither."

This touched and broke my heart at the same time.

I continued to seek the Lord and had a desire to know Him more. I had a talk with Him one day that went something like this:

"Lord, I hear you saying to think big, to pray big, to work big, that big yesses mean big sacrifices and big prayers mean big blessings. My tiny sufferings run parallel to my small, self-focused way of thinking. I want to live big for you. I say yes to you, that I want to live big for you, and I do not know what this means for my suffering or sacrifice, my 'I'll do anything, but please don't ask me to _____.' Maybe it is good that I don't know what that is because if I did, I might not have the courage to say yes. You are an incredible God who knows my name, who knows my fears and my limitations, who knows my desire to know you even more. You know my heart. Nothing matters except the faith I have in you. I commit to following you wholeheartedly, no matter what."

I had a very perplexing dream one night that my husband and I were on an empty roller coaster. I was in the front car, and he was four seats back. As the coaster curved back and forth very slowly I was singing, "Wherever You Lead I'll Go" to the Lord. Why would I be in front? Wasn't I supposed to be behind my husband? I was to submit and follow him. Why was he behind me? I wondered if this meant that I was leading him spiritually. Was this a vision that I was to be a catalyst in him having a relationship with the Lord?

We celebrated our 21st wedding anniversary with dinner out and time alone at home. It was typical for my husband to stay up much later than me every night to unwind and watch TV. I went to bed but got up a few hours later to get something to drink. I walked into the kitchen and found him on the phone. I knew instantly that it was *her*. I asked him who he was talking to and he wouldn't answer me. I attempted to snatch the phone out of his hands, but was only successful with half of it. *There was no doubt. How could he do that, especially on our anniversary?* It showed that he was not emotionally attached to me like I thought he was or should be. Every time we were *"here"*, every time *she* entered our marriage, it chipped away a little bit more of who I was.

Why was he doing this? Was I not good enough for him? I was a helpful, supportive, loving wife. I took care of him the best that I could by cooking a sit-down meal every night, washing and ironing his clothes, and keeping the house and kids going, in addition to working full time. Why was all that not enough? How could God bless the business if this was still taking place there?

I was on the battlefield fighting fierce demons from hell. They had been coming from all directions, testing my will and my strength. It was definitely a battle in the spirit realm. I knew I was supposed to believe Truth, but I could not put the training and battle plans into action. These demons were very strong and held nothing back. I was wearing down fast. I did the things I knew to do, but the demons were neither backing down nor giving up.

I envisioned myself at the top of a very high hill standing next to God. My clothes were torn, my face dirty and sweaty, my hand barely able to clasp my sword. The tip of it was on the ground because I did not have the strength to hold it up anymore. I took one look at God and said, "I am tag teaming with you. You go in for me. I'm done."

In my spirit I felt Him respond, **"You know you didn't have to stay in that long. Why did you wear yourself out so? I have been here ready to go in because this battle is not yours. It is mine."** Then God descended the hill.

A few days later one of satan's demons got in my face and put the tip of his sword at the edge of my nose, taunting me to raise my sword and fight another battle. My husband called to say his truck had broken down and he needed me to come get him. When I arrived, he was parked in front of *her* house. He needed to "drop off some money", he said. I mustered up the strength and said to myself, "No, this battle is not mine either. I will not fight this."

This isn't to say that I was not struggling. My mind was constantly consumed with *this relationship*. A pit was my new home. I wore myself out mentally, and it was so bad, that there wasn't anything I could do. It was so hard, that it was easy to accept what God was handing me. Peace. Power. Him. I pressed my way through the madness and buried myself in the busyness of my daughters, and somehow, I was still breathing.

God frequently spoke to me through nature. A very cloudy, gray, any-minute-gonna-rain sky showed me my struggles, trials and hard knocks of life that covered me incessantly. A spot of blue sky near the sun showed me hope, and that God was above it all. Hope is where the Light is.

If there was no money to pay all of the bills on time, there certainly wasn't money for anything extra. An ignored septic tank problem result-ed in raw sewage coming back up into the house from both commodes. Out of the bathrooms and onto the carpets into the hall and bedroom. A tree limb fell during a recent storm and put a hole all the way through the roof tile. Weeks went by. I finally climbed on the roof and covered that hole with a plastic trash bag and bricks. Yearbooks were distributed one day in middle school, and my baby girl got passed over. She did not get her yearbook when everybody else did. Her money did not get turned in. Her daddy didn't write the check. I called home one day to check on the girls and couldn't get through to them. The phone had been disconnected. He hadn't paid the phone bill.

I wanted to give up. I was empty. I was doing what I knew to do, but it wasn't enough. I latched onto 2 Corinthians 1:8 and made it mine: *"I am under great pressure far beyond my ability to endure, so that I despair even of life. In my heart I feel the sentence of death. This happened that I might not rely on myself, but on God, who raises the dead. He has delivered me from such a deadly peril and he will deliver me. On him I have set my hope that he will continue to deliver me as those who help me by their prayers."*

Soon afterwards I felt like God reached down, picked me up and put me down somewhere away from my circumstances. I realized my place with Christ was not contingent upon where someone else was in his or her heart, or if my bank account had enough money in it. God knew the desires of my heart. As bad as I wanted to walk spiritually with my spouse, God wanted it even more. I had been allowing my husband to change who I was and hinder who I was to become. The only One who I wanted to change me was God, and He wanted me to be who He created me to be.

Home Base

*"Since we are surrounded by a great cloud of
witnesses, let us throw off everything that hinders
and the sin that so easily entangles and let us run
with perseverance the race marked out for us."*

HEBREWS 12:1

Lydia and I continued our pursuit and desire to know God more.
We went from one study to the next, learning and growing and
being transparent. We had a unique opportunity to talk about what we
were reading throughout each day as we taught school together. We
spurred one another on through emails and chats and reminders of
Truth.

She knew about the struggles in my marriage, and I knew about
hers. We were both working hard at surrendering to the Lord. I wanted
to do that no matter what it took. I felt that my husband's transformation was depending on it.

It was about this time that I wanted Lydia and Allison to meet. They were experiencing some similar struggles, and I knew that they could get encouragement from one another. Lydia told of the miracles God was performing in her own home and it gave Allison hope. Allison knew her friend, Rosemary, could benefit from our time together and they invited Grace. The five of us met at my house, and over waffles and coffee, HomeBase was born. It was a place of security, encouragement, and accountability, a spiritual "safe house" to be Godly women despite our circumstances and relationships, and to allow God to change those relationships out of our willingness to surrender. We met every other Saturday for four years. A marriage was saved. Our teenagers got critical resources when needed. Hope was kept alive. Perseverance was spurred on.

It was unlike anything I had ever experienced. I went from sharing my heart and soul with one person to sharing with four, and it was reciprocated. It was a very safe, yet sometimes hard place to be. Hard because we knew we had to be open and real, and sometimes doing that was uncomfortable. But, it was also like getting redirected and spiritually charged up in order to survive.

Grace shares the impact HomeBase had in her life, and how God has shown Himself faithful…

When I went to HomeBase, I was greeted with love and warmth and waffles. There was no agenda; sometimes we would share a devotion, a journal or a struggle. There were times when one of us might be "needier" than the others, and sometimes our whole time together would be spent ministering to that one person, and that was okay. It was a place

I felt accepted, loved and not judged. It was easy to be real and transparent.

But the thing I remember most about HomeBase was when Bethany and Allison were going through their hardest times, they encouraged me to stick it out and to stay in my marriage. I wanted to be on the bandwagon with them. But they told me that if their husband would make the slightest attempt to try and change, to pursue them, or to get help, it would have made all the difference in the world. My husband was doing that.

I never gave up hope. I envisioned the outcome that I wanted and one that God would be glorified by. I was more afraid of disappointing God than I was in disappointing Rick or myself. But, even though I had this hope, I did not want to keep living like I was living. I prayed and asked God to empty me. I begged him to change me and to change my husband.

I had a lot of hurt and resentment and bitterness towards Rick. I was so angry that our sons were participating in dangerous and illegal behavior and all they got was a slap on the wrist. I was the drill sergeant, and Rick was their friend. He didn't want to deal with it, and I was desperate to save their lives.

Rick and I went to counseling. I was broken. We didn't seem to be getting anywhere. I really wanted a divorce, but I was more afraid of being disobedient to God than I was at wanting my own way. So I hung in there and cried out to the Lord to change me, to change Rick and help me love him.

You see, I always thought I was right. I soon realized I had trespassed on the hearts of those I love the most because although I had done things for the right reasons, I hadn't done it with love. In other words, I may have been right, but I did not handle things in the right way. That was big. God revealed to me that I had crushed my family along the way. I had criticized and wounded Rick by not lifting him up and encouraging him.

We continued to face challenges with one of our sons, and it put tremendous pressure on our marriage. I eventually had to give my husband an ultimatum because he still did not want to deal with the problems we were facing. Because our son continuously chose inappropriate behavior, he was no longer welcome in our home. This was a very low point for me.

It became evident that our son was not the problem, but had amplified it. I started looking for a job so that I could position myself financially to be on my own. After working for a year, I began to struggle with fatigue, pain, depression and anxiety. God knew my motives were not pure, and I found myself physically exhausted.

I came across 2 Corinthians 2:6-11 which says, "The punishment inflicted on him by the majority is sufficient. Now instead, you ought to forgive and comfort him, so that he will not be overwhelmed by excessive sorrow. I urge you, therefore, to reaffirm your love for him. Another reason I wrote you was to see if you would stand the test and be obedient in everything. Anyone you forgive, I also forgive. And what I have forgiven-if there was any-thing to forgive-I have forgiven in the sight of Christ for your sake, in order that Satan might not outwit us. For we are not unaware of his schemes."

I was convicted that I needed to forgive Rick. I prayed Psalm 51:10, "Create in me a clean heart, O God, and renew a right spirit within me." God began to do a work in my heart. I grew to respect him after he welcomed my sister into our home for a short time. We started doing little things together and for each other. There was a sense of renewed hope and tenderness for one another. Over time, God gave me new eyes and a new heart for my husband, and He let me see Rick as He saw Rick. My husband saw my respect and genuine desire to meet his needs, and he responded so wonderfully. Trust began to build, and we really desired to do things together.

God was so faithful to restore my marriage, but He didn't stop there. For years I had lived with the inner turmoil of anxiety and fear. I had a fear of rejection, abandonment, and letting people down. I found it very difficult to stay home alone and would often get so anxious that I had to leave and go some-where. I had to keep busy. Other people thought my life was perfect. It was in no way perfect. But, the Lord has taken away my fear and anxiety! Now I am so content to be at home. I am happy being still, quiet and spending that time with Him. I find joy in making our home a place my husband will want to come to at the end of the day.

> The Lord has been so good to us. Rick often tells me that he wishes he had loved me like he does now our whole marriage. And I feel the very same way.
> ~ Grace

On New Year's Eve my little family and I decided to drive up to my parents' beach house to get away and to celebrate. We were getting ready to go out to dinner and my husband's cell phone rang. He was not near it so I answered it. The caller hung up. I researched the number and determined that it was *hers* and confronted him about it. He claimed not to know why she would be calling. Really?

I wanted to be set free from *this* once and for all. After rattling off a long list of my thoughts and fears to him, all I got was "I will try harder because I am obviously not doing a very good job." The results? An "I love you" as we headed out to dinner. A "You look nice" and "I'm glad to be here with you." Seriously? I wanted to scream out, "This is NOTHING. I should be hearing these things anyway!" His comments didn't come anywhere close to what I needed. They may have taken the edge off, but my fears were enormous and those were gnat-size, feeble attempts to reassure me. All it took was a "silence all" on his cell phone to send me back to the deepest, darkest corner of the pit.

After we returned home, I brought up *the situation*. Emotions flew and he said he was entitled to talk to whomever he wanted. I told him he was not, and that I wanted him to leave. I guess that got his attention because he then said he would take care of it, in his own way. One month later I had nothing to go on. No proof of it being taken care of, not even mentioned. Six months later, nothing. I had absolutely no knowledge of, or to what degree, *the problem* still existed. This was humanly impossible to live with day after day. God's strength was the only thing getting me through. I poured myself out to the Lord, begging, pleading for Him to show me what was happening. God told me I was not supposed to know anything now. I think that maybe if I did, I would have given up and been gone. God impressed upon me that I was to stay right where I was. I needed to trust God, not my husband, for all my needs. I had to keep my eyes on God.

I lived on a spiritual and emotional roller coaster. The not knowing was eating me alive. I prayed that Light would uncover the darkness. I prayed for the scales to be removed from my husband's eyes. I had been miserable for so long and tried my best to hide it to protect Claire and Liz. Nonetheless, it wasn't hidden from my husband. I was accused of being moody and not myself. There would be days we would not utter one word to each other. I felt desperate and irrational. I told God I couldn't live under lies and secrets and betrayal. I tried so hard to give God time to handle it. I tried so hard to trust Him. Some days I was successful, and some days I was not.

I was still digging in His word and attempting to apply what I was reading to my situation. I had to shift my focus from my husband and his relationship to that of myself. I was the only person I could change, the only person I had any control over. My "to do" list consisted of the following: stop nagging, stop pointing out negatives, have a quiet spirit, be positive, praise God and exert my mental energy on positive things.

God continued to give me the strength to persevere with spiritual nuggets, such as the following from Arthur Christopher Bacon, "I can still believe the day will come for all of us, however far off it may be, when we shall understand; when these tragedies that now blacken and darken the every air of heaven for us will sink into their places in a scheme so august, so magnificent, so joyful, that we shall laugh for wonder and delight."[3] I had to cling to this hope. I had to trust God that everything would be okay.

A Plan

"For I know the plans I have for you," declares
the Lord, "plans to prosper you and not to harm
you, plans to give you hope and a future."

JEREMIAH 29:11

God often makes a way. A solution presented itself, something that would solve all of my problems.

Over the years, my husband considered selling his jewelry store, but it never came to fruition. It seemed as though someone was now very interested, and plans were being made to make it happen. What would he then do for income? Where would he work? He was tossing around the idea of selling real estate. He would make a profit from the sell of his business to go toward retirement. For *every* reason that I could think of, I wanted him to do it. Our whole house was a buzz of excitement and anticipation of what our future held.

Things were in place for him to do a 90-day Going Out of Business sale. The first day of the sale would be HUGE. The newspaper ran a big ad, the radio station aired pre-recorded commercial spots, and someone would be there recording footage the first day for future advertising. We were expecting a very large turnout and extra help was needed. The girls and I would be there to help wait on customers.

We were sitting at our dining room table one Sunday afternoon working on a massive mail out. I was addressing envelopes, and the girls were stamping and stuffing them. It was a family effort. After the girls got up, the two of us were sitting there. He said to me, "You know, Saturday, the first day of the sale, is very important. I expect to have hundreds of people in the store that day. We need help. *She* would be invaluable. How would you feel about *her* helping for a day?"

"How would I feel?" You can imagine my response. Whatever you are thinking right now, I said it.

I wanted to be done with all of it, once and for all. This was my ticket. No store = no *her*. I agreed. The battle in my mind was fierce the week approaching that Saturday, but somehow I managed to do it. Somehow I managed to be in the same room with her and wait on customers with great composure. I wore a brand new gray pantsuit, black heels and pearls. I glanced across the store from time to time at my precious daughters and thought, "I'm doing this for them. I'm doing this for him. I'm doing this for all of us."

The day was a success. The day after was not.

"Everything is dependent upon the success of this sale the next three months. We have to do well in order to have money to live on. I need experienced people to be able to handle it. I need her to help for the duration of the sale," he said.

Eighty-nine more days. I wondered, "Is this my, 'I'll do anything, but please God don't ask me to _____.'" I felt that God was allowing this to be in my face so that I would deal with my trust issue once and for all. I had to trust God above everything else, no matter what. I knew I was to honor God in this and that He would take care of everything, despite what others did to me or their lack of concern for my feelings.

How could I agree to it you may be asking? I had to die to self and put the needs of my husband above my own...his need for business success and financial stability. I also wanted to show him that I loved him. I put his needs above my own sense of well-being. Above my own sanity. Above my own physical, mental and emotional health. But, most of all, we had an agreement. I told him I would agree to it if he would end his relationship with her once and for all at the end of ninety days...to break all ties and communication with her. He said he would. This would be worth enduring three months of mental and emotional torture.

Knowing that she was at work with him everyday consumed me. It was a constant tug of war between trusting God and living in a depression. I set out on a mission of searching for proof that he was having an affair. He covered his tracks because he knew I was looking, but it didn't stop me from trying. And, try I did. One Friday afternoon he called to say he would be working late. I protested, but to no avail. I decided to ride up to the jewelry store and walked in as *they* were closing down for the day. I went into his office and found an R rated movie in his computer. I took it. I guess I ruined their Friday night plans.

I was pretty much in emotional shut down mode for weeks, but managed to take care of my many responsibilities. Lydia was right by my side, hurting with me, pointing me to Jesus, and praying me through.

I was still desperate to find proof in order to confront him head on and make him admit he was having an affair. I went to extreme measures and came up with nothing. It was beginning not to matter anyway...he was having an affair of the heart and had broken mine in two.

When there were 27 days left of the GOB sale, I reminded my husband of the agreement we had. I point blank asked him if he was going to end his relationship with her on the 31st and he said, "I'm not agreeing to anything. I don't like being told what to do, and you are sticking your nose where it doesn't belong. You are trying to control my personal life." His personal life? How absurd. I was his personal life.

I could not function. I could not eat or sleep, sat paralyzed at home, and was an emotional basket case. I wanted to die. For weeks I had been trying to trust God and my husband, while knowing she was at the store. I felt misled about her being there for a day, then twelve weeks and now what seemed indefinite. I could not live with this and began to have thoughts of dying. My feelings toward my husband were love/hate. I didn't want to talk to him on the phone because he acted like everything was okay. When he didn't bother to call me, I was disappointed and mad. I told him again and again the whole thing boiled down to security, and he chose to ignore that. One of the things a husband was supposed to do was protect his wife and that included her heart. He broke mine and continued to do so by choosing this *friendship* over my need for security, well being and peace of mind. I did not feel cherished, safe or valued. I verbalized all of this to him. It was serious. My imagination allowed me to explore ways to end my life, which I told him about. I also spoke of divorce. I told him I couldn't live like this any longer. I had been living like this so long that I wasn't myself anymore. I was slowly dying, little bit by little bit. Who was going to rescue me, if not him? The only one I could think of was myself, with the strength of God Almighty, and He promised to do that.

"It is God who arms me with strength
and makes my way perfect."

PSALM 18:32

I threw myself into the Lord. My bed was covered with books, my Bible, CDs, journals and sermon notes. I spent everyday like this-- searching, seeking, and surviving. I begged and pleaded for God to convict and change my husband. I knew God did not like divorce, nor did I want one. I married for life, and I loved him. I also didn't want my daughters coming from a broken home.

Prompted by a sermon, I journaled the following:

"With my God I can scale a wall. Rise to the occasion; do the thing. It does not matter how it hurts as long as it gives God the chance to manifest Himself in my mortal flesh. I am sanctified, set apart, and I am to separate my spirit from my emotions." God was showing me how to do this. My husband and I didn't have a spiritual relationship so I had somewhat of a head start.

But the "rise to the occasion; do the thing" could have meant stick it out, don't push, let God handle it. I sobbed out to God that I could not do it, to take this cup from me, that His will be done. I did not have peace or even the stability that I could survive under these conditions. I knew I was to submit to God's will so that He could work through me however He wanted. I just didn't know what that was.

Expect the Unexpected

"The Lord is my light and my salvation- whom shall I fear?"

PSALM 27:1

By nature I am a fixer and a fighter. I will search for ways to remedy a problem, and I will stand up for what is right. I would not let it rest. God spoke to me with a quiet nudge one morning and said, **"This is about you and where you are; it is not about your husband, what he is doing, what he is not doing, getting proof, etc. Rise up out of the wreck, daughter. Tell him where you are, and leave it at that."**

A few days later I told my husband that I loved him but that the love was buried so deep that I could not feel anything. I was broken and brokenhearted. I could not get past this so I guess we needed to part ways. I never dreamed I would say those words, and it was not what I wanted. But, even more did I not want things to be as they were. He told me to go ahead and make myself miserable if I wanted to. I'm sure he didn't believe I would go through with it.

I lost the desire to fight that week. Something in me died. But, I felt God's amazing comfort and security. The following morning I read this excerpt from Oswald Chambers' *My Utmost for His Highest* entitled "The Delight of Despair":

It may be that, like the apostle John, you know Jesus Christ intimately. Yet when He suddenly appears to you with totally unfamiliar characteristics, the only thing you can do is fall "at His feet as dead." There are times when God cannot reveal Himself in any other way than in His majesty, and it is the awesomeness of the vision which brings you to the delight of despair. You experience this joy in hopelessness, realizing that if you are ever to be raised up it must be by the hand of God.

"He laid His right hand on me…" Revelation 1:17. In the midst of the awesomeness, a touch comes, and you know it is the right hand of Jesus Christ. You know it is not the hand of restraint, correction, nor chastisement, but the right hand of the Everlasting Father. Whenever His hand is laid upon you, it gives inexpressible peace and comfort, and the sense that "underneath are the everlasting arms" (Deuteronomy 33:27), full support, provision, comfort, and strength. And once His touch comes, nothing at all can throw you into fear again. In the midst of all His ascended glory, the Lord Jesus comes to speak to an insignificant disciple, saying, "Do not be afraid" (Revelation 1:17). His tenderness is inexpressibly sweet.[4]

The next day we went for a walk and my husband told me that he loved me and didn't like to see me all torn up and that "parting ways" was the craziest thing he has ever heard me say. He said I was making more of it than there was and my vivid imagination was the problem. He commented that he could not be closing the store without her help and this made him more indebted to her than ever before.

He said my actions were to get vengeance from them being involved 15 years earlier. I told him that what happened 15 years ago was the foundation that everything was building on. He said, "People change. Haven't you changed in 15 years?" I replied, "Thank God, yes I have."

I wrote him the following morning that nothing got settled, and I still couldn't live under it, especially knowing he was so indebted to her. I had to get out from under it one way or the other. His response, "It is business. I have an emotional relationship with you. How long does somebody have to pay for something? I am home every night. You shouldn't let people steal your joy. You haven't been happy for some time. You don't have fun. You are always so serious."

At this point I could not think straight. I did not know what was truth or reality. I was living as if all my fears and fantasies were in fact true. Every time I talked with him I got confused and frustrated. However, I had seen one thing clearly. I had to let it go completely. God had me, and God had my husband. God would show me whatever I needed to know and see.

The last day of the GOB sale came and went. The lady who bought the business took over, but my husband remained to help her transition into running it. A few weeks later he rented office space for his new "real estate business" and took all of the paperwork from the GOB sale that needed to be processed. He took *her* along too. "Just because the business sold does not mean that there isn't a lot of final paperwork to do," he informed me. I wasn't surprised. In fact, with fear and trepidation, I was expecting it.

A few days later, Lydia and I took our students on a field trip to Washington, D.C. I called my husband at the end of a busy day of sightseeing. When I asked him what he was doing he said, "Painting the office." I questioned if he was alone and he said no. *She* was helping him paint. "Shouldn't I be the one helping him paint and decorate his new office?" I wondered. It sure seemed like it. It was just one more chunk out of the little bit that remained of who I was.

As I searched for answers, I was reading about keeping God alone in my inner circle while keeping everyone else outside of it...children, husband, friends, etc. We have to stay focused on God and keep him first. I recognized that I couldn't be the Bethany that God created me to be and realize my passions and my dreams. My life, thoughts, feelings and heart were all intertwined with a husband who did not honor and cherish me. I didn't know who I was. I spent a lot of time trying to please him. He dominated me because he wanted things his way, and I gave in because I loved him and wanted to please him. By moving him out of the inner circle, I could find out who I was. God was the only one I should ultimately please. I had to say yes to Him, in spite of the cost.

Tearing Away

It was summer. School was out. Can I tell you how excruciating it was to watch my husband walk out the door each morning to go to the "office" knowing she was there, just the two of them? It was unbearable. My stomach dropped each time he said goodbye. I couldn't eat. I couldn't sleep. God was impressing upon me that I was to stand up in that inner circle, to live, to be set free and to live out my passion. I couldn't do that under the current situation with my husband. I had tried everything. I begged. I pleaded. I ignored the situation. I forgave. I embraced it for his benefit. I cried. I held him accountable. Despite trying everything, I didn't make any headway, but I did come to these conclusions: One person cannot save a marriage. A marriage cannot survive with three people in it. I had to save myself.

I wrestled with God over and over with regards to divorcing my husband. I'm talking soul-searching, mind-boggling, and gut-wrenching conversations with Him. "God, you hate divorce. Why haven't you stepped in? How can this be the answer? It doesn't make sense! What about Claire and Liz?" I prayed for God to move the mountain or move me. All I can say is I didn't get specific answers to my questions, but what I did get was peace.

God never ceased to amaze me with the timing of His Word in my continual pursuit of Him. The following excerpt is from *Praying the Names of God* by Ann Spangler:

Scripture is full of the promises of God, and when we respond to him faithfully, nothing can prevent their fulfillment. That holds true regardless of circumstances. Think for a moment about Abraham's circumstances. God had promised his descendants would be as numerous as the stars in the sky and the sand on the seashore. But how could that promise be fulfilled if the first star, the first grain of sand- if Isaac himself- were destroyed? Ironically, the promise was fulfilled precisely because Abraham was willing to act in a way that seemed contrary to its fulfillment. Had Abraham refused to obey God, he as might well have forfeited the incredible blessings that followed.

When it comes to the things God has promised us- wisdom, strength for our trials, a way out of temptation, and fullness of life- our obedience is key. No matter what the circumstances, we need to realize there is no limit to God's power to do what he says- if we believe and obey.[5]

This was incredible confirmation that I was walking in God's will despite the ever-seeming contradiction to my reasoning and to my dream.

I learned from parenting and from teaching that you don't make a threat unless you are willing to follow through with it. I prayed and considered the next step I was willing to take to show my husband I meant business. The Lord spoke to my spirit, **"Put your marriage on the altar."** "I thought I had already done that, Lord?" **"Not completely."** That next step would be for the girls and me to leave home. I secured a location for us and came home and told my husband. His response was, "What if Claire doesn't want to go? Why do you want to do this to yourself, to the girls and to me?" I replied, "I don't. I told you I couldn't live like this anymore, and you left me no options. I'd rather spend the rest of my life alone than continue living like this." His response? "Do you want something to eat?"

I was thankful that God offers strength to the weary. *"Even to your old age and gray hairs, I am he, I am he who will sustain you. I have made you and I will carry you; I will sustain you and I will rescue you." Isaiah 46:4.* Boy, did I ever need rescuing. Even in the tearing away, I was empowered, and I knew it was coming from God. This gave me the strength to carry through and take the next step. It is important to note, however, that deep down, at any given moment, I was willing to forgive him, reclaim my marriage, and live happily ever after.

I was living in a "checked out" state and just going through the motions. I had said so many times that this had to be "all or none". I tried so hard to make it "all". It looked like it was going to be "none". How in the world my husband came home from work every night as if nothing was wrong was beyond me.

"I can't keep doing this, Lord." **"You put your marriage on the altar, but I want it all. Put Claire and Liz there, too."** Just before he left for work one morning, I told my husband that I was going to talk to the girls and tell them we were separating. He asked me not to and walked out the door. I immediately called him on his phone, and he did not answer. I got in my car and drove to his office. I had to knock on the door until he unlocked it, and when he did, I saw *her* sitting at her desk across from his. The phone rang, and when he answered it, I asked her if I could speak to her outside. I figured if he wasn't man enough to make this right, I would. I had purposefully avoided speaking to her prior because I knew he needed to be the one to address the relationship, not me. I wanted it to be genuine remorse and then a pursuit of our marriage and me.

I was very candid with her and told her that I was not comfortable with their "friendship" and that it was affecting our marriage. I told her that it was on the brink of ending. She said my husband did not want a divorce. This made me aware that he was speaking to *her* about the state of our marriage. I went so far as to tell her that he was not willing to end their relationship, and that it was up to her to remove herself from his life. She went inside, got her purse, and left the office.

When I went back inside, I was riddled with accusations and blame. He had a way of projecting and pulling things out of nowhere to use as ammunition that focused on me. In my soul searching over the previous months, I realized that I was not the person he married. I had changed. I had grown by leaps and bounds spiritually. He even used this against me. "You are a different person. I can't handle the baggage of your Christian friends, Christian books, Bible studies and continuous Christian music everywhere. It is over-kill sometimes." It was in that moment, looking across the room into his eyes, hearing the words that criticized my faith and my walk with the Lord that I realized I didn't know who he was anymore. I asked him point blank if he was going to end his relationship with her and he replied, "No. There is nothing wrong with her being a friend. You are trying to control me and you are imagining things. I used to be emotionally affected by this, but not anymore. You are just trying to bully your way into my personal life."

I left and was dumbfounded as I reflected on what he said. Was this my *husband* saying these words to me? So now I am supposed to minimize what I do spiritually? Be self-conscious about what I am reading or listening to? Die spiritually like I have died emotionally and mentally? I knew. I knew that I knew that I knew it was over. There is no way I would ever diminish or change my relationship with the Lord in any way. How dare he insinuate such a thing.

Talking to my daughters was a very difficult thing to do. I told them their daddy was having an inappropriate relationship that he was not willing to let go of. I resented him for causing them such pain. They did not see it coming and were caught totally off guard because we protected them from our relationship issues. Realizing he was not willing to fight for me was devastating. Realizing he was not willing to fight for our family was excruciating.

I really struggled with causing my girls so much pain. This was the reason that I put up with so much from my husband for the last seven months. I did not want them to have divorced parents. I did not want them coming from a broken home. But, I could not continue to live like I had been living. I wasn't going to make it. I finally accepted the fact that they would be better off having a single mama than a dead one.

My Big God

"However, as it is written, No eye has seen, no ear has heard, no mind has conceived what God has prepared for those who love him, but God has revealed it to us by his Spirit. The spirit searches all things, even the deep things of God."

1 CORINTHIANS 2: 9-10

A "Deeper Still" weekend ladies' conference with Beth Moore, Kay Arthur, and Priscilla Shirer was the buoy that the Lord gave me to cling to. It was the fuel I needed to make it a few more weeks.

The lady who bought the jewelry store agreed to pay a lump sum up front and then a certain amount each month. After a month or two, she was talking about filing for bankruptcy. My husband took the store back so he wouldn't lose what was left of it. He opened it under a new name but still had the *same ole employee.*

A new school year began and so did the decline of my Granny's health. She was diagnosed with lung cancer. I had one daughter starting college, one starting high school, and I was slap dab in the middle of working on a graduate degree.

Our twenty-second wedding anniversary was also approaching. We had always shared a fondness for "The Andy Griffith Show" so we decided on a weekend getaway to Mt. Airy, NC where it was filmed. We ate, walked around, and did the usual sightseeing. There was a ravine of distance between us. The conversation was shallow and awkward. It seemed there was nothing left between us. Nothing left *of* us. When we returned home I asked my husband one more time to go to marriage counseling. His reply? "I don't need to go to a marriage counselor. I have a perfectly good head on my shoulders." To top it all off, I found out he was giving her money and paying her bills, all while I was scraping money together to buy back-to-school clothes.

It became evident that my Granny could not care for herself any longer. She would need someone to stay with her, and I knew it couldn't be me. The following weekend, overwhelmed and exhausted, I had to get some help.

God showed up and showed up big in my life. I woke up Saturday morning and went to my Granny's. God began to meet needs I didn't even know I had. I was not able to sit still long enough to make phone calls to get sitter coverage for her. I had a long list, but couldn't get to it. Allison called and said, "What time can I relieve you?" I knew I probably wouldn't go anywhere, but it would free me up to get things organized. I spent eleven straight hours doing so. In the meantime I watched my girlfriend bathe my Granny, kiss her forehead and apply her nursing skills to survey the situation. Allison talked me through Hospice Care, Home Health Care, when to know about seeking emergency attention, etc. I was overwhelmed because I didn't know what to do for my Granny and God sent me a Hospice Nurse/Home Health Care nurse/Oncology nurse/daughter-of-a-cancer-patient in my precious friend.

I ended up with sitters, but too many different strangers were going to come through the door, and my Granny never would have kept them all straight. Within the hour, God used my brother, Matt, to send me two full-time people to care for her. People we didn't know spoke of praying for us and asking if Granny knew Jesus; complete strangers showing the love of Christ. My heart was touched by people reaching out to us. Grace, my HomeBase girlfriend, offered to sub for me at school. I knew she would take good care of my students, as well as getting my own kid to and fro. Through my dependable prayer warrior Rosemary, I felt carried through those last several days because she kept me high and lifted up, right there in the face of Jesus. It was pure joy to juggle a schedule with my daddy so that *everybody* could make it to church on Sunday. God is so faithful.

I also experienced the love of God in additional sibling connections that only times like those reveal. How did my brother, Daniel, and I go from taking Granny's bed down and moving her into a hospital bed, to playing "Whose Line Is It Anyway" in her driveway with a rose bush stem? The same way my brother, Ron, and I talked so spiritually deep that our heads spun as we sat on her back porch and discussed how to continue to seek Him in our lives.

I was amazed that God was working in such big ways. I was immediately reminded of Lydia coming to see us when Granny broke her pelvis a few years back. Granny had no patience for our silly game of charades when my "snarl" almost made Lydia pee in her pants and Granny chimed, "I'm going to bed." Lydia also took care of the looming graduate homework assignment hanging over my head.

God continued to work that Sunday when Dixie called to say "I'm going to Granny's with you." We had our own "church service" and God crystallized HUGE things for us. We are not to say, "Let God be in control," but instead, "Let the God in me be in control because Christ lives in me." We have to move to the level of faith where we tap into the power that Christ made available to us through His crucifixion on the cross. Most Christians settle. We can have so much more if we only claim what is already ours. God was preparing my heart for that next level of faith, and I was ready.

The next Monday I took off work so that I could meet with the Hospice nurse. Early that morning my daddy called to say he was following my mama to the ER in an ambulance. It appeared that she had had a stroke. I had a melt down. After getting myself together, I woke Liz up to tell her. She asked, "Is she going to be okay?" I immediately made the choice to claim that Power and said to her, "We are claiming right now by the blood of Jesus that, yes, she will be alright." A few days ago I would have said, "I don't know, we have to pray for her and ask God to give the doctors the wisdom to know how to help her." The difference was claiming through His blood that there would be victory, but this time I felt it, believed it, lived it and walked it out. Driving in the dark to the emergency room, I played a CD from our choir that Claire bought for me on Sunday, and with my hand lifted out of the moon roof, covered with spiritual goose bumps, I was praising God. Not until later did I realize that I was praising Him in a storm. God sent my mama home from the hospital that very day.

I had recently been asked by a sister in Christ to describe myself as a teacup and what kind of teacup that would be. My response? I think I am a daintily painted teacup that has nicks and scratches from all that it's gone through, but you can't bear to throw it away because it is still useful, still has a purpose, still holds some Good Stuff.

This cup runneth over with the love and faith and hope and power of a Very Big God who showed up in the middle of the storm of me slowly losing my Granny.

The Inevitable

⟋⟍

*"We were under great pressure, far beyond our ability to
endure, so that we despaired even of life. Indeed, in our
hearts we felt the sentence of death. But this happened that
we might not rely on ourselves but on God, who raises the
dead. He has delivered us from such a deadly peril, and he
will deliver us. On him we have set our hope that he will
continue to deliver us, as you help us by your prayers."*

2 CORINTHIANS 1:8b-11

The day after placing my Granny on Hospice care, I found myself sitting in my car in my carport. I called the store. When he
answered, I could hear *her* in the background. He said it was the radio.

*"Abraham bound his son Isaac and laid him on the
altar, on top of the wood. Then he reached out his*

*hand and took the knife to slay his son. But the angel
of the Lord called out to him from heaven, 'Abraham!
Abraham!' 'Here I am,' he replied. 'Do not lay a hand
on the boy,' he said. 'Do not do anything to him.
Now I know that you fear God, because you have
not withheld from me your son, your only son.'"*

GENESIS 22:9-12

Ann Spangler writes:

Why would God ask for such a sacrifice? Because he knows there
is no other way for us to learn that he is God. When we put something on the altar, sacrificing it to him, we acknowledge two
things: that he is God, and that we are not God. This is the worship we need to offer, the worship that will allow us to experience
his provision for our lives. Each of us will be faced with Abraham's
dilemma, perhaps many times in our lives. In our case, it won't
be a matter of physically placing a child on an altar, but it may
mean placing a child in God's hands, forswearing our tendency
to be a little god to that child, trying to control her universe and
to keep her safe. If not a child, then something else- a relationship, a career, a gift, a dream. Whatever it is, if we offer it to God
as Abraham offered his only son, we will begin to know God as
Yahweh Yireh, the Lord who provides everything we need.[6]

**"You've put your marriage and your daughters on the altar, but
you haven't raised the knife. Raise the knife."**

"Okay, God. And you're going to provide a ram, right?"

I knew it was best for my daughters if my husband was the one to leave instead of us. I called my brother and asked him if he would come to my house and change the locks on my doors. I had an indescribable peace. I drove to check on my Granny and came back to find him changing the first lock. I got out of my car and greeted him with a smile and my head held high. I felt empowered. I went in and packed my husband's bags. I packed EVERYTHING. As I was loading the car in the early afternoon, it started raining. By the time he was changing the last lock I was ready to go. I hugged him, thanked him and left.

I was driving down the interstate in a tremendous down pour. My windshield wipers were on high, and I could barely see the flashing tail-lights of the semi truck in front of me. I drove slowly. I was nervous, yet confident. I went a little further and noticed the rain easing off. I looked in my rear view mirror, and it was so dark that it looked like nighttime. I looked in front of me and saw blue sky and sunshine. The rain had stopped.

"You have made it through the storm."

The peace was unimaginable. My nerves were completely under control. I *knew* that this was what I was supposed to do.

I pulled into the parking lot of his business and parked next to his truck. I placed all of his belongings inside and went into the jewelry store. He was the only one inside. I told him that I packed his bags, changed the locks on the house, and didn't want him to come home until he could be the husband he needed to be.

His response, "Did you pack my medication?"

I said, "Yes" and placed a one hundred dollar bill on the counter for his hotel room. He said he didn't need it. I said, "Good, because I will."

As I was pulling out of the parking lot, *she* was pulling in. I looked over my shoulder and saw her walking into the store with lunch. God had cleared the store of her and any customers so that I could talk to my husband in private. God also knew I needed to see with my own eyes that she, indeed, was still around. This was a gift. God knew I had to be sure.

The minute I pulled back onto the interstate there it was. A rainbow. I drove all the way home under a full rainbow… God's promise and reminder that He had me. There are no words to fully explain the abundant peace and incredible power I felt. I called my brother to tell him I was okay. He had been sitting in his truck praying over me the whole time I was gone. He also prayed over every room in my house before he left.

Telling my daughters that I had packed their daddy's bags and had the locks changed on our house was the hardest thing I have ever done in my life. They were stunned. I did my best to comfort them. I gave them their new key and the promise that I would be with them through this no matter what. I didn't have any answers, but I shared with them my hope and peace. My heart broke for them. This part of my heart would never, ever heal. However, my spirit knew that God had them.

That October I experienced the love of God in a powerful way. My colleagues helped me out with lesson plans and graduate homework, as I was so preoccupied with both a dying Granny and a dying marriage. I waited for my husband to call to say he was sorry and that he was coming home. He did neither. Lydia lovingly reminded me to stay on the road, under the rainbow- where Truth and Life and Love live- where promises are made and promises are kept. Psalm 28:6 says, *"Praise be to the Lord, for he has heard my cry for mercy. The Lord is my strength and my shield; my heart trusts in him, and I am helped. My heart leaps for joy, and I will give thanks to him in song."*

I felt a huge hedge of protection over my emotions like never before. I prayed for God to show me His will and to make the way smooth with no obstacles. I had one conversation with my husband in the five weeks he had been gone. I knew he was stubborn, but to go five weeks with no attempt to initiate conversation or healing of any kind? He put everything off on me, and obviously had no desire to take care of me, to love me or to make sure we were even okay.

I continued to miss what we once had. I woke up every morning alone with the realization that he did not love me enough. It was uncomfortable answering questions from people who asked where he was. They were dumbfounded because we did such a good job living behind the veil. It was difficult watching the hurt in my daughters' eyes as they, too, felt unworthy of being fought for. My husband lived in denial and blamed me for packing his bags.

"Sometimes agreeing to God's will means saying no to the right to make it happen as we'd like and saying yes to trials and hardships, heartache and suffering, terrible loss and great pain. I needed a submitted heart that kept on believing…even when it hurt," writes Joanna Weaver.[7]

The Lord pressed upon my heart in a very clear, direct manner.

"Enough is enough. Cut her loose."

"But Lord, what about the ram? You are supposed to send a ram!"

"It's over."

I dropped Liz off at a movie theater one Friday night and pulled over in the parking lot. I remember sitting in the dark. I remember dialing his number. I remember telling him, "I want a divorce." I don't remember what he said. I just remember he didn't fight it. He was willing to let it all go, to let me go, to let our family go. *She* meant that much to him. It didn't make sense. It hurt so badly.

And just like that, the end of a twenty-two year marriage was over. It was not what I expected, but I had peace. It was not what I wanted, but I trusted God. He was carrying me. I felt alive and free, but worried greatly about my daughters and how this was affecting them. I would be okay, but they would have to live with this for the rest of their lives.

Soon after, I met with a lawyer, and the papers were served. It was an easy process. Too easy.

A week later, on November 23, 2008 at 3:30am, my Granny went to heaven. At her graveside, encircled by my family, I shared my heart...

Indelible memories are etched in my mind. Memories of weekends and summers spent on Lynnwood Drive with Roy and with Granny. To this day, I like to hear the noise of a baseball or football game playing in the background of a room, especially on Sundays. It is soothing and peaceful and reminds me of them. As I woke up to the smell of Roy frying bacon, I would join Granny by the big window to see what critters were out having breakfast. She taught me many species of birds. At lunchtime, I thought I was so cool going out with a picnic that she fixed for me, which consisted of a cheese and mayo sandwich and Coca-Cola in a mayonnaise jar. Her lap was my favorite place to sit and her bed, my favorite place to sleep. She was the best back scratcher in the whole wide world, which was the last thing I thought about before falling asleep. I made sure I taught Claire and Liz her technique. Saturdays were spent in the kitchen baking cheesecakes, chocolate mousse cakes, and cheese rolls. Nobody could outdo Granny when it came to making divinity. She taught me her secret to homemade milk gravy, but mine has yet to turn out as well as hers did. Afternoons were spent at the pond, and I thought it was so clever of Granny to fish with kernel corn or balled up bread when we were out of bait. We ended the day by feeding the raccoons sliced bread with peanut butter.

Granny has always been one of the most optimistic people I know. She saw the glass half full and would always point you in the direction of seeing the bright side of things. You always received her opinion on a matter as she freely offered advice, but she was also okay when you did not take it. A few days ago I learned that Granny and Roy used to pack a picnic lunch and hit the road with no particular destination in mind. They would ride the countryside together, sometimes crossing into the next state. (No wonder I'm so fond of picnics.) In very recent years, Granny still enjoyed getting in her car to drive the country roads of Morgan County. When she couldn't drive anymore, she and I would take off with no particular destination, eating our cheese crackers or McDonald's hot apple pies. I could not believe it when she told me this summer that she earned her pilot's license. This would have been back in the 50's. That same grit and determination lasted her entire life. She was strong and she was tough. I saw this spunkiness just last week. She had gotten to the point where she was not talking much so we tied a bell on her bed so she could call for help. She hated that bell and told us so with a glaring look as she pulled it off. Her outspokenness and independence was evident until the very end.

I received a text from my husband to say he was sorry to hear about my Granny. He couldn't even make a phone call.

The one thing that I could do for my girls was to stay in the only house they had ever known. I wanted them to have some sense of stability. As I've mentioned many times, we were not in good shape financially, and now I was left holding the bag alone and facing a financial crisis. How would I make a house payment that was almost half of my paycheck? Our house was average size but our payment was high due to refinancing with large cash advances that went into the business. Both of my girls have December birthdays, and Christmas quickly followed. I had little experience handling finances, but I called my mortgage company and explained my situation. I had to complete a financial history and breakdown of my living expenses. The representative commented about my tithing and said that it was good to do, but at certain times the money might have to be used for something else. I said, "No. I don't believe that. God has been faithful and will continue to be faithful with regard to my finances." I kept that as a priority, and God indeed showed himself faithful! I was able to refinance my house and drop my mortgage payment by several hundred dollars a month. The new payment would not be due for two months so I was able to use that money for birthdays and Christmas. This was huge for me to successfully tackle on my own. It gave me a sense of confidence and relief. God was so faithful.

That December was bitter-sweet. We were a family steeped in tradition, and my girls struggled despite carrying on those traditions. The proverbial elephant in the room was bigger than our Christmas tree. I hurt for them. I had to find the balance of being there for them and not constantly asking if they were okay. I had to learn to let them talk about the divorce when they needed and wanted to. When they weren't doing that, I was fearful that they were bottling it all up and not dealing with it in a healthy way. I got lost in my daughters and in trying to figure out who I was. I had spent so much time and energy being a wife and trying to save my marriage that I had lost myself. Though I know it needed to happen, I still couldn't believe I was going through a divorce. Like Liz said to me one day, "I've always looked at families that were divorced and thought, we are the lucky ones, and now here we are." I felt like I had a "D" stamped on my forehead and hated that I had failed my daughters.

I found myself thinking about what I had spent the last few years searching for…wanting someone to want me. I knew I had healing to do and it was way too soon to be pursuing that desire. I wanted the girls and I to have plenty of time to heal. I wanted them to be okay. But I was alone and lonely.

The new year brought a new friend that I corresponded with via email. I put my hope in the Lord, not necessarily in this man. I trusted the Lord would give me the desires of my heart. Jesus was my hope.

It was nice to have someone to chat with, laugh with and get to know. My divorce was still not final so it was strictly a correspondence friendship. It really is true that when you marry, you become one. I was feeling the effects of the tearing away. I questioned why I wasn't enough. I couldn't understand why he would throw it all away. Why wouldn't he fight for our family? I was relieved to be out from under the oppression, but I still struggled. I was teaching, in graduate school, overseeing my Granny's estate, and taking care of my daughters and myself.

Spring was approaching and so was my desire to meet this new friend. He was fun and gave me butterflies. We had a lot in common. My interest in him and feelings for him had really grown in the few months we emailed and chatted. We were counting down the days to the divorce finalization. It arrived and so did the weekend we were to meet face-to-face. We had lunch, and the next day I received an email saying it was best that we not continue our friendship. He knew. He knew it was too soon and my heart was moving way too fast. He was a Godly man and smart enough to see that I had more healing to do.

However, I was devastated. Rejected again. It took three months for my heart to settle and to accept the fact that I had a lot more work to do.

Part 3

A New Normal

Trading Ashes for Beauty

*"I have come that you may have life
and have it more abundantly."*

JOHN 10:10

The light blue walls became oatmeal neutral. A new, flat screen TV replaced the small, old TV that sat on top of a broken console TV. The fireplace was insulated, closed and covered with sheet rock. Sentimental keepsakes sat on its new glass shelves. The red hand-me-down sofas were replaced with a chocolate brown sectional. Even the ceiling got a fresh coat of paint. My den underwent a transformation. My house was becoming a home. Friends that came over couldn't believe the change in the feel of the house. It exuded warmth and peace, and they noticed. I noticed, and it was wonderful.

The Lord had blessed in a great way, and I told Him I wanted to give that room back to Him. I opened up my home to host a summer Bible study for twelve women. We dove into *Esther- It's Tough Being a Woman* by Beth Moore, and I grew by leaps and bounds. It was a soothing balm to my lonely, rejected, betrayed heart. I knew I had spent the last year of my marriage trying to do everything I could to save it, but that didn't mean the process was easy. I felt lost.

Esther was faced with a crisis situation where there was no neutral position. She had a decision to make, and not doing so would mean personal loss and not fulfilling God's purpose in her life. This directly applied to me in that my broken marriage came down to my walk with Christ being criticized. I was trying to live out who I was in Christ and was verbally attacked and belittled. I could not live for Him and keep Him in a closet at the same time. A warring concoction of anxiety and despair overtook me as I wrestled with whom I had been early in my marriage and whom I became after knowing Christ. I had to make a decision that I was God's child first and foremost. I had to muster the strength to raise the knife on my marriage. I would identify myself with God, even if it killed me. If I didn't die, life as I had known it with my husband was dead anyway. There was no way back so I stepped into the unknown with my veil off.

To be crucified with Christ was to be more alive than I had ever been. Beth Moore pointed out in the study of Esther that God does not leave things dead. A theme in Esther talked about what God can do when we decide to obey and, "'If I perish, I perish.' Esther was called to obedience, not to figure out how it was all going to shake out. Any time He calls us to die, His purpose is to reveal larger life."[8] I was encouraged by this but continued to question why God didn't provide the ram- a substitute for my failing marriage, a way to save it.

I had my fleshly, weak moments. The Lord was teaching me to die to my emotions and pull away from them. He wanted me to use my head, to seek Him for wisdom, and to bank on what I knew. I was to remember His faithfulness. It was a tug of war though. I hate to admit it, but I was falling into the trap of wanting a man to fill the void I was experiencing. What if I'm alone the rest of my life? I knew I would never live my abundant life if I lived in fear. But, I wanted someone to share my life with. I wanted a companion. I wanted to be loved again. I knew it would take time, and all I got was one day at a time. Sometimes it felt like forever.

I learned that God is never inactive. When He puts a hold on something or calls us to wait upon Him, something is up. Things on earth are coming into the will of the things in heaven and we have to trust Him. Waiting is exhausting, but Scripture says, *"...but he who waits upon the Lord will renew their strength,"* Isaiah 40:31. Beth Moore pointed out that we will lose our strength when we wait upon the event, on the thing, or on the person. When I am waiting upon the Lord, my strength will be renewed. Habakkuk 2:3 adds, *"For the revelation awaits an appointed time; it speaks of the end and will not prove false. Though it linger, wait for it; it will certainly come and will not delay."*

My experience in seeking the Lord with all my heart has never left me void of what I needed spiritually. In fact, He has always shown and given me more than I could have imagined. The Esther study was one such occasion. I highly recommend it. There is no way I can include all of what the Lord did in my life and in my heart through this time spent with Him. The spring and summer after my divorce was a time of rest and celebration of life and God's hand on my life. I could see His hand in every step in my journey- the steps of pain, the steps of provisions, and the steps of peace. This providence allowed me to totally trust Him and have faith in Him for my future.

Along with that providence, I felt His presence. I felt it in the lullabies of frogs in my backyard, in blistered, bandaged feet of my fifteen-year-old missionary, in shimmering lights on my bedroom wall from a swimming pool full of new friends and youngest daughter. I felt it in lightning bugs who met me after dinner each night, in continuous laughter with my college-bound first born, and in my Jesus-loving Esther girls.

God was with me, and also went before me, just like on the morning I had to attend a hearing before a judge for the first time in my life. As I began dressing, I simultaneously donned anxiety because this girl had been raised to respect her authority figures, and one wearing a robe deserved a little extra. A loose end needed to be tied up regarding my grandmother's estate, and former conversations with this particular court's office left me intimidated and on edge. This judge held the power to give me the document I needed, or not.

I drove to the courthouse coaxing the butterflies in my stomach to settle down. In thinking about being before a judge, I couldn't help but compare this to being before The Judge one day. Is this how people will feel? Not even close. I thanked God right then that I won't have to experience that because Christ made a way so I won't have to. I was to meet my lawyer's assistant at the courthouse. How will I know who he is? "He is 35 with straight, combed back hair," I was informed. Confident and nervous I walked in the building and found the security screening intimidating enough. I didn't know what to expect, I just knew I would be sworn in and asked questions by the judge. What if I said something wrong?

It was not difficult to spot my legal representative because he was the only one in the building. He introduced himself while holding my file containing the necessary paperwork and asked me if I had any questions. "No," I said, "I will just follow your lead. I have never been before a judge, and I don't know what to expect." We entered her chambers; he sat beside me, and then presented my case. I felt confident with him at my side. He had assured me it would be simple, and it was. Fifteen minutes later I was on my way home with the document I needed.

I thought about how Christ prepared my way for heaven just as my lawyer had gone before me in preparing what I would need for the hearing; how having trust and faith can make fears dissipate; how Christ will present me to the Father one day and because of His precious blood shed for me, I will be able to stand before God with confidence. *"But if anyone does sin, we have one who speaks to the Father in our defense--- Jesus Christ, the Righteous One. He is the atoning sacrifice for our sins, and not only for ours but also for the sins of the whole world." 1 John 2:1-2.* I thanked God for His atoning sacrifice. For His love, His forgiveness, His grace, His mercy, and His blessings. He continued to provide exactly what I needed.

Summers had always allowed for rest and rejuvenation, catching up on to-do-lists, and soaking up my girls. This one was no different, and we were growing even closer. Having three brothers and being the only girl, I had always been so glad that Claire and Liz had a sister, and now I was beginning to feel as if I had gotten two. We could be found dancing in the kitchen, advising each other on our wardrobes, and going on shopping excursions.

One such adventure left a fantastic memory on my heart. We were shopping when Liz picked up a cream-colored ceramic apple and said to me, "Isn't this so cute? You should get this Mom. It would look cute in the den" At first glance I thought, "Um, no, I don't really like it." The more I thought about it and the more I looked at it, it grew on me. I put it in the shopping basket. "You are NOT going to buy that are you? That is the ugliest thing I have ever seen," chimed Claire. "All these pretty things and you pick THAT?" she continued. This caused me to give the apple a second thought while looking into the big, brown eyes of my latter-born child with an expression that said, "Are you putting it back?" I laid it back in the basket, which continued the debate followed by Claire's comment of, "If you put that in the den, I am going to get it and hide it. Just because it is on clearance doesn't mean you have to buy it. When have you ever seen a cream-colored apple?" She tried everything. Liz looked at me and grinned. As we checked out, the giggles surfaced and Claire thought she would give it one last try. She said to the cashier, "Don't you think this is ugly?" The cashier looked at the apple, looked at her, looked at me, and then said, "Yes. It is." By this time I am in stitches, and nearby customers start looking at us. There is no doubt in my mind about whether to purchase it at this point. I had to have it. Not because it was a one-of-a-kind, cream-colored ceramic apple on clearance, but because it was the source of fun, laughter, differences of opinion, and an afternoon of love shared between a mother and her incredible one-of-a-kind daughters.

Summertime also meant taking our annual trip to my parents' beach house. While looking out over the water, I reflected on the previous summer with my husband and daughters. We were miserable. Tired of the same, old patterns. Tired of where we were and getting nowhere.

God had moved in the past year to deliver me from the blanket of oppression and from the secrets that infiltrated my marriage. The mourning, weeping, fasting and wailing was over. I was beginning to experience the second half of my reversal- one of happiness, joy, gladness and honor. Oh, how I wanted God to be glorified and honored.

"Then this city (Bethany) will bring me (God) renown, joy, praise and honor before all nations on earth (people in her life) that hear of all the good things I do for it (her); and they will be in awe and will tremble at the abundant prosperity and peace I provide for it (her)." JEREMIAH 33:9.

I had gone from living in black and white to living in full color. I felt alive, and I was thriving. It was as if I could see again. Hear again. Feel again. I seemed to be more in tune and paid attention to details... the ocean's horizon, the hungry cry of seagulls and the bright, blue sky. That is how I noticed him while looking out over the balcony...

Clad in his red, white and blue outfit and licking the icing off of his cupcake, the seven-year-old boy said to his cousin, "Isn't this the best day ever?" As fireworks popped in the night sky and his sun-kissed cheeks revealed leftover icing, I couldn't help but marvel at his positive outlook. He undoubtedly had a day of fun in the sun and topped it off with two hours of fireworks on the beach.

"The best day ever." It would be so good if we could say that every day- to have that kind of positive outlook with each day that God gives us. Unfortunately, some days are not "best days". Some days are riddled with all kinds of struggles and trials that make it a day we want to be over with quickly. So, with the ebb and flow of good days and bad days, we embrace the good ones. We look up instead of down, sing out instead of remain silent, praise Him instead of pout, and let everyone know of His faithfulness. We turn our palms up and accept His grace and mercy, and we bask in His glory. We allow our hearts to fill with His love and spill over with thankfulness. We stand in awe of His sovereignty and His majesty. *These days* are the "best days ever". *"This is the day the Lord has made; we will rejoice and be glad in it." Psalm 118:24.*

Still trying to shake the stigma of divorce, fully accepting the fact that my marriage ended, and feeling like I failed God and my daughters, I struggled. And right there on the beach, with tears streaming down my face, I read the following excerpt from *Three Weeks with My Brother* by Nicholas Sparks:

I hung up my shoes *(my marriage)* for good, feeling sadness and--strangely--relief. With the exception of breaking a school record that still stands after nineteen years, *(my beautiful daughters)* I'd failed to reach the other goals I'd set for myself. But despite the fact that running *(marriage)* had been the defining force in my life for the previous seven years, I knew that I'd survive without it. I'd given it my best shot, but it wasn't meant to be. And if I had to do it all over-- and fail to reach my dream again-- I would. When you chase a dream, you learn about yourself. You learn your capabilities and limitations, and the value of hard work and persistence.

When I told my dad *(God)* about my decision to stop running *(to divorce my husband)* he put his arms around my shoulder. "Everyone has dreams," he said. "And even if yours didn't work out the way you wanted, it doesn't make me any less proud of you. Too many people never really try."[9]

God was so good to give me that. It spoke to my heart and settled me. I knew that I had not just thrown my marriage away. I had given it my all; I had tried everything. I honored God in it, and He moved. Being able to say so and knowing God loved me brought me peace. Trusting His faithfulness brought me peace. Healing was a process, and it would take time.

Fall soon arrived and so did saying goodbye to my firstborn child as she moved away for her last two years of college. Decorating Claire's dorm, checking out the campus and filling her fridge and pantry were fun and exciting. Saying good-bye was not. I cried all the way home. I was proud of her and excited for her, but I missed her already.

Liz had a hard time as well. She was starting high school, which was a pretty big transition in itself. Now her sister, who she clung to tightly over the last year, was leaving. She had always been so resilient, and she continued to amaze me with her inner strength. Now it would be just the two of us.

First Place

"Yet the Lord longs to be gracious to you; therefore he will rise up to show you compassion. For the Lord is a God of justice. Blessed are all who wait for him."

ISAIAH 30:18

A year had passed since the separation and divorce. Part of discovering who I was meant trying some things I had always wanted to do. One of those things was dancing. I snagged a girlfriend and off we went to the local Christian singles dance. I had no idea what I was doing, but I just put myself out there. This was a very big deal for me because I had always worn the hat of being the "go to" person. Be it the oldest child syndrome, being a teacher, or being a mom, people needed me to have it together and looked to me for answers. I lived my whole life needing to know what I was doing. Stepping out on that dance floor without a clue was both humbling and freeing. Every time I went, I learned more and more. It was fun and liberating; I was having a blast!

As I was out on the floor slow dancing one night, a large, heavy thunderstorm came through. I thanked the Lord for the dance and for the pouring rain, for speaking to me deep within and letting me know, letting me see. I thanked Him for teaching me to admit the things I did not know and reminding me to keep the veil off. Freedom is there.

I was not looking for a date. I just wanted to dance. However, I was soon swept off my feet and pursued hard. The desire of wanting to be with someone never left my heart, so maybe I was ready to test the waters. It felt wonderful to be sought after and to be wanted, especially having been rejected. I thought it best to ease into this, both for my daughters' sake and my own.

At least that was the plan. To ease into it. But it didn't really happen that way. I was so hungry for affection, love, adoration and pursuit that things moved way too quickly. I let my guard down and allowed this relationship to take center stage in my life...a place I vowed to save for God alone. There was also a good bit of conflict in this relationship, but I tolerated it because I wanted to be wanted so badly. I finally faced the nagging feeling that this relationship was not right, and after many months, much prayer, and seeking the Lord, I ended it.

I was heartbroken. I remember being distraught, emotional and grief-stricken. What I learned from feeling this way was that I had more healing to do. I'm talking God-seeking, soul-searching healing. I turned to Him for my rescue.

One of the first things I learned in my new quest came from *Captivating* by John and Stasi Eldredge. As women, we long to be loved, pursued and romanced. God made us that way. Our human nature is to fill this with a man. God wants us to fill it with Him. "What would it be like to experience for yourself that the truest thing about God's heart toward yours is not disappointment or disapproval but deep, fiery, passionate love? This is, after all, what a woman was made for."[10]

I often wondered, "Didn't God create man and woman to be together? Aren't we creatures of relationship?"

Stasi Eldredge says, "The Great Love Story the Scriptures are telling us about also reveals a Lover who longs for you. The story of your life is also the story of the long and passionate pursuit of your heart by the One who knows you best and loves you most. God has written the Romance not only on our hearts but all over the world around us. What we need is for Him to open our eyes, to open our ears that we might recognize His voice calling to us, see His hand wooing us in the beauty that quickens our hearts."[11]

Then it began to shift. I started to get it. This insatiable, innate drive we have to be filled in our soul cannot be filled by a man. That is asking too much of him. He was not created to do that for us. Only God can fill the God-shaped hole that He made in each one of us...male and female alike.

I guess getting to the place where all that I had was Jesus made me realize that He is all I need. When my mate was removed, when I didn't have anyone else, it was easy to put Christ first. I remember trying to make that shift in my marriage. I had put everything in my relationship with my husband first for so many years. I just invited God along for the ride. Could I truly keep God first if and when I did meet the man He had for me?

The second thing I realized is that I don't have to be "fixed" or healed before I can live, so I kept dancing. It was my lifeline. And so was S.A.S.

Single **A**gain **S**isters. Whether through divorce or being widowed, I had a slew of girlfriends who were all single. We decided that instead of sitting at home alone on Friday and Saturday nights or falling into the trap of becoming "man chasers", we would hang out together and do things that were healthy for us. Over several years, we went rafting, were in Bible study together, went to Sunday school and church, to the beach, to concerts and to theater plays. And we danced. Every Saturday night. And we breathed life into the place. We had the best time laughing and dancing and living. Dancing seemed to be the theme for my new life.

Four of us clung together a little more tightly and met on a weekly basis. Wednesdays at 3:00 would find Eden, Patricia, Jenna and me at a local restaurant sharing our days and our dreams. We would talk out parenting struggles and dating again. We each found ourselves in new territory, and it was so good to have sisters who empathized in our current season of life. We would laugh and cry and encourage one another. It was a sweet time that we looked forward to. We needed each other. That was for sure.

Claire was thriving at college and decided to study abroad in Spain. Liz was plowing her way through high school and struggling with math and physics, so I hired a tutor to get her through. She was very active in her church youth group. Her social life was busy like mine, and we soon encountered a problem. On the occasions she didn't have any plans for the weekend, she wanted me to be home with her. I didn't want to be home alone so I would make plans ahead of time to be with the S.A.S. girls. I struggled because I knew this was not how things were supposed to be. I was supposed to be home with my husband while my teenage daughter flourished in her high school social life. It was backwards, and I felt bad. I wanted what was best for my daughter, but I had to make sure I was taking care of myself as well. We learned to communicate and plan ahead. With God's grace and patience and understanding from both of us, we eventually found that balance.

Why is it that so much of our journey is filled with baby steps? We trust God and claim that "He knows the plans He has for us," but those plans seem to always come in little steps. It's like playing "Mother, May I?" As kids we didn't like it when one of us would get "five elephant steps" and the next would get "three gigantic steps" and when it was our turn we heard, "Take four baby steps". Ugh. Not fair.

The truth is the baby steps are necessary for our spiritual foundation to be firm and rock solid. We are more like Christ when we wait, and in the waiting, we trust, and in the trusting, we grow and come to realize that His timing is perfect. We get further down the path and look back and see that He *did* know what he was doing! In John 13:7 Jesus said, *"You do not realize what I am doing, but later you will understand."*

This knowledge doesn't make it easy, but doable. Hebrews 6:12 tells us to *"imitate those who through faith and patience inherit what has been promised."* Some of the inheritance God has promised each of us can only be received through faith and patience. So when it is our turn and we hear Him say, "Take three baby steps" we will say, "Father, May I?" and we will take those baby steps with trust and faith that we WILL reach Him.

In the "slow and steady" motto I was attempting to live, I was thriving with my girlfriends and with my daughters. I loved going to high school games to watch Liz cheer, and I enjoyed driving to Athens to spend the weekend with Claire.

College football games were definitely an experience and it was "Saturday in Athens, GA." Game day. The sidewalks and streets were crawling with fans decked out in red and black. The stands were full and speckled with the team's colors. Cotton candy hanging from poles made its way up and down the steps while the game clock ticked down to kick off. It was Saturday in Athens. "If you bleed red and black, please stand to your feet and welcome the Redcoats as they make their way onto the field," said the announcer. Big Bad Bruce was proudly escorted between the hedges while adoring fans clamored for a picture. The feature twirler added her fourth flaming baton to her routine, and anxious fans hoped their faces would be the next ones shown on the big screen. Sitting on a cold metal bench with my first-born, I was proud.

Proud that she got to experience college life at a school with incredible team spirit and proud that she worked so hard to get here.

Then...there was Sunday in Athens. The streets were not as crowded as we drove to Watkinsville Baptist Church. We sipped coffee and waited for the heater to come on, chatting and looking for a close parking place. We entered the sanctuary and the musicians were making their way onto the stage. It was Sunday in Athens. "If you are here to worship Jesus Christ, please stand to your feet and let's praise His name," said the worship leader. The guitar, the box drum, the flute and the mandolin rhythmically ushered in the Holy Spirit. Lyrics fell onto our hearts, and we were reminded to "praise God from whom all blessings flow". Sitting on the pew next to my first-born, I was proud. Proud that she was faithful in attendance, but even prouder that she had a heart for worshipping our Savior. Proud that she took *me* to church and when *she* introduced *me* to *her* friends, *she* seemed proud of *me*. I think the tables were turning. It marked the beginning of our mother-daughter relationship shifting to that of best friends.

In my quest to stay close to Him, God rewarded me with something I had long been searching for.

Henry Blackaby in *Experiencing God* wrote about the account of the death of Lazarus from John 11:1-44:

John reported that Jesus loved Lazarus, Mary and Martha. Although Jesus received word that His good friend was sick and at the point of death, He delayed going until Lazarus died. In other words, Mary and Martha asked Jesus to come help their brother when he was sick, and Jesus was silent. All the way through Lazarus's final sickness and death, Jesus did not answer. They received no response from the One who said He loved Lazarus. Jesus even said He loved Mary and Martha. Yet he did nothing. Lazarus died, and Mary and Martha went through the funeral process, preparing his body, putting him in the grave, and covering it with a stone. Still, God's silence continued. Finally, Jesus said to His disciples, "Let's go."

When Jesus arrived, Lazarus had been dead four days. Martha said to Jesus, "Lord, if you had been here, my brother would not have died". Then the Spirit of God began to help me understand something. It seemed to me as if Jesus said to Mary and Martha: "You are exactly right. If I had come when you asked, your brother would not have died. You know I could have healed him, because you have seen Me heal people many times before. If I had come when you asked Me to, I would have healed him. But you would have never known any more about me than you already understood. I knew you were ready for a greater revelation of Me than you had known before. I wanted you to experience that I am the Resurrection and the Life. My refusal and My silence were not rejection. They were opportunities for Me to disclose to you more of Me than you had ever known."[12]

And finally, there was the "ram" I had been looking for.

God wanted me to know him more...His provisions, His love, His faithfulness. He knew I was ready for a greater revelation of Him. God could have saved my marriage, but he gave my husband free will to choose. God wanted me to experience Him on a far deeper level than I had ever known, and more of Him than I have ever known was: incredible provisions, being able to make ends meet, refinancing my house, Christmas and birthday money, turning my house into a home, strength and peace, coming out of oppression and being set free, dancing, amazing friends and hope for a better someone who would take care of me. He wanted me to be the Bethany He created me to be.

I kept waiting for the ram. When one didn't come, I had peace and saw God's favor and blessings in every area of my life. And then, when the time was right, He was faithful in showing and giving me exactly what I needed...the greater revelation of Him.

Part 4

Euphoria

Dance

"Lord, you are my God; I will exalt you and praise your name, for in perfect faithfulness you have done wonderful things, things planned long ago."

ISAIAH 25:1

The crisp air of fall always brings a sense of excitement and renewal. I lived for dancing on Saturday nights. The S.A.S. girls filled our table and we laughed, talked and danced for hours. Though we had many new moves under our belt, there were always more to learn. Such was the case with a sweet guy who attended regularly. He asked me to go into the foyer so he could show me the steps to The Sway, which we later danced together.

The following Saturday night, Jack was asking me to dance a little more often, and by the end of the evening, he asked for my phone number. We talked for hours on the phone for days until work called him 300 miles away. On the morning he left, he dropped by my house with roses, put his arm on my shoulder and prayed for my daughters and me. It blew me away. No one had ever done that with me.

When we talked during that week, he asked me if he could take me to get ice cream on Saturday night. "But it is a six-hour drive home, and you have to work in Alabama Monday morning," I reminded him. He said it would be worth it. After working twelve hours and driving for six, it was close to midnight when he arrived home. The ice cream places were closed so we sat out in the pasture under the stars and ate coffee ice cream out of the carton with two spoons. To our astonishment, we witnessed a moon bow, which is a bright ring around a full moon. He drove six hours back to work the following day. I couldn't believe he went to that much effort and sacrifice to see me. He certainly got my attention.

To my surprise Jack said he would be making the drive home again on another weekend to attend the singles dance for Halloween, and that when I arrived, I should look for… Batman.

The S.A.S. girls decided we would all dress up and go as princesses. We met at Patricia's house and got dressed together. We were like teenagers laughing and cutting up and doing each other's hair. We made a grand entrance wearing our floor-length gowns, white gloves and jeweled crowns. Batman swept me off my feet that night and never let me go. Talk about feeling like Cinderella! I don't think my feet ever touched the ground as I floated across that dance floor.

Jack also got my attention a few months later when he was sitting at his piano and played *Master of the Wind* by Joe Hemphill. He said it was his story that spoke about "what the good Lord had done for him." The lyrics told of God calming the storms of our lives and making the sun shine again.

With tears in my eyes, I knelt at the piano and hugged him. It was my story, too. Jesus came to me as a friend in the biggest gale I had ever experienced. He calmed the storm, figuratively and literally, and He was making the sun shine so bright in my life. Jack told me he spent many nights standing in his front yard under the stars praying that God would send him someone special. He felt like his prayers were being answered after many years of praying and patiently waiting.

Dance lessons with my *favorite* dance partner filled the following months. We spent time getting to know each other with bow shooting, hunting, attending church, meeting family and hanging out with friends. We shared chai teas, secrets and dreams. God was so good to give me someone to share his creation with. We also shared His Word... reading it and gleaning from it. His Spirit...feeling His presence in our midst every time we were together. His Peace...that surpasses all understanding. As the layers were peeled away, I saw such a Godly, thoughtful, genuine, caring, tender soul, and I was smitten.

On one of our Wednesday afternoon outings, my girlfriends and I sat outside a local restaurant and made a list of criteria we were looking for in a mate. After spending time with Jack, I was steadily putting a check beside each and every one of the items on that list.

When you fall head over heels for someone, as we seemed to be doing, the relationship takes center stage. Even though I had a desire to keep the Lord first place in my life, my heart was turning somersaults, and fears crept in. I recognized that God was at the center of our relationship and later came to understand that He created us for relationship, and that it was okay to be investing my heart, time and energy into getting to know Jack. My fear was for my daughters, especially the one still living at home who had a front row seat and had to share my time. In other words, I was falling in love, but needed to take it slow...a difficult thing to do.

I remember being in angst over Liz accepting Jack and our relationship. This is where my S.A.S. girlfriends were my sounding board and source of encouragement. It was all about keeping a balance, being open and honest and giving her time. Sounds easy. It wasn't. After many months I knew in my heart that God had given him to me, and I had a peace about spending the rest of my life with him. I would verbalize this in a round about way, and he felt the same but was guarded. He wanted to be sure. I was bound and determined that I would NOT tell him I loved him first. No matter what. I wanted him to lead in our relationship.

Cooking dinner had been something I have always done, and it seemed that "the way to a man's heart is through his stomach" was ringing true. Jack would stop by on his way home from work, and I would have a plate ready. One night after he ate, he was standing in the kitchen hugging me and said, " I...love............sweet potatoes." Sweet potatoes!?!?! SWEET POTATOES?!?! I was mad. No, more like disappointed. Of course I didn't say anything to him, but I sure did whine to my girlfriends. Why was it taking him so long to say those three words?

Somewhere in the first year that we dated I did hear those three words. It was worth waiting every minute to hear them, from him, first. I knew, that I knew, that he meant them, and I didn't ever have to wonder if I coerced or influenced him into saying them.

After graduating from college, Claire accepted an internship with *Southern Living* magazine, which meant she would relocate to Birmingham, Alabama. We went for a weekend visit to see where she would be living and working. Her new best friend and roommate was seventy-five years old and did Zumba! Claire knew no one in this big city, and I watched with awe as she chased her dream despite the fear, discomfort, loneliness, and uncertainty. It took guts. She would be a five-hour-drive away, the farthest from me she had ever lived, but I knew how to find her...straight down I-20, heading east.

Liz was well into her senior year of high school and "under the gun," which meant I was too. I found this note on the kitchen counter one morning:

Mom,

These next few weeks are going to be <u>CRAZY</u>. I need you to do a few things for me:

* Call about hemming my dress
* Write bio by Sept 23
* Write insert for yearbook by Sept 29
* Keep me sane- everyday
* Put these on your calendar:
* Senior Project Sewing classes Sept 16, 23, 30
* Arts in the Heart -National Honors Society Sept 17
* GCSU college visit Sep 23-25
* See You at the Pole Sept 28
* Fifth Quarter Sept 30
* SAT on Oct 1

The week of the 26th will be time for you to be the soccer mom you always wanted to be. Beware.

Liz

And to our delight, her tutor was still hanging around. Thomas finished his job getting her through math and physics her junior year, and then asked her on a date. She agreed, and he was gently pursuing her.

Words cannot describe the angst that Liz felt with regards to her future. She did not have a peace about starting college the following fall. While all of her peers were getting acceptance letters to this university or that university, she shuddered at the thought of sitting in a college classroom. But, the pressure to go was huge. Everyone expected it. She had been approached to teach English to kindergarten students at a Christian school in Siguatepeque, Honduras. The seed was planted several years ago on previous mission trips to Honduras. The thought both scared and excited her. She didn't know what to do.

Jack's love, encouragement and support for my daughters was enough to melt any gal's heart. He was kind and gentle and sweet. He prayed *with* them when something was going on and prayed *for* them each night. He was there to listen to senior project presentation practice and discussions over Honduras missions and college decisions. He kept us giggling, and he kept me smiling.

I have learned something very important. Some people wonder if God causes bad things to happen or they may ask, "Why did God do this to me?" This is what I know. God never intended for us to live with death, disease, struggles, sorrow and pain. Sin entered the world and changed His plan. He chooses to rescue us from some of these things. He also chooses to use some of these things for our good and His glory. Though I begged God to save my marriage, He chose to rescue me instead. He gave me the freedom to live an abundant life and be who He created me to be. He traded ashes for beauty.

He also uses trials to show and teach us things. Jack had jaw surgery, which resulted in his teeth being banded together for six weeks. A few days after the procedure, he ended up in the hospital with pneumonia. I was right by his side. In fact, the nurses let me sleep in the patient bed next to him in his semi-private room. They felt sorry for him. About the third day into the stay, he was getting worse instead of better. Fever stayed with him, and he appeared to be giving up. He started talking about "not making it". This scared me to death. We were weary. Late in the night, in that dome lit room, I just held him and cried and prayed. A few days later he went home and made a full recovery. Some time passed before he shared with me that it was in that moment in the hospital when we cried together that he knew I truly loved him. It was the assurance he had been looking for. God uses difficult circumstances to open our eyes.

Despite living on cloud nine, I was miserable professionally. Teaching middle school was hard. Teaching language arts in middle school was extremely difficult. I was an "all in", "above and beyond" kind of teacher, and after 21 years of teaching, I was exhausted and burned out. In addition, the times were changing. Much of our energy was spent testing, collecting data and documenting. We had to prove what we were doing instead of getting in there and actually teaching. If our scores were in the exceeding range, it wasn't good enough. They were always wanting more. I left work feeling defeated every day.

Once again I knew I was not the Bethany that God created me to be, this time in my job. The Lord had given me this kind of clear discernment before, so I knew, that I knew, it was right. I had a peace about leaving the profession. Oh, don't get me wrong, with this announcement, I had people looking at me like I was crazy! "What about your retirement?" "How will you make this kind of living doing something else?" "You have 21 years in, why not make it to 30?" I could not make it one more year, let alone nine. Even though I had peace, I questioned making such a life-changing decision. I had to be guarded against the world and the things of the world and people's opinions. They meant well, but some of them were voices of reason as opposed to voices of the Spirit and what God was calling me to do. This was an opportunity for further surrender. My future was wide open with regards to an income, finances, insurance, marriage, etc. I could have gotten focused on one or more of these huge issues, but I chose peace, God's sovereignty and His timing in it all.

The hardest part was leaving my best teaching buddy and friend behind. I thought about staying a few more years until Lydia retired, but I couldn't even do it for her, and I knew God was calling me away from education.

My girlfriends and teacher friends joined me for a "She's Quitting" party, and they shared in my relief and excitement to be moving on. Jack supported me. My daughters could not believe I was resigning. I guess they had never known me as anyone else other than a mom and a teacher. It took them some time to accept the fact that I was "done". Liz graduated from high school, and I "graduated" from middle school education. I didn't have a plan, I just believed in the Plan Maker.

And my little drummer who marches to her own beat? She decided to make a Kingdom difference and committed to teaching Honduran children about English and about God. Her high school friends knew what they were doing when they voted her "Most Likely to Change the World." She would do just that.

Shells and a Shovel

~

*"Now to him who is able to do immeasurably
more than all we ask or imagine, according to his
power that is at work within us, to him be glory
in the church and in Christ Jesus throughout
all generations, for ever and ever! Amen."*

EPHESIANS 3:20-21

It was time for our annual Litchfield, SC family beach trip. We were able to coordinate everyone's schedule, which was becoming increasingly more difficult, and had everyone there. Jack, Thomas, Liz, Claire and I had deep sea fishing plans, sun to soak up, and rest to get. It is a very relaxing, not-so-commercial place to visit and, having vacationed there for 20 plus years, we knew all the great places to go and traditions to continue: puzzles, sleeping til noon, fried grouper sandwiches, fireworks, and new coloring books. Exposing Jack and Thomas to our favorite get-away made it even more enjoyable.

I have a fondness for sunrises, sunsets and full moons. The gang was talking about getting up the next morning to see the sunrise. Yeah, right. They are rarely up before noon. I made my mental plans to get up and go to church.

I woke up the next morning and had missed the sunrise, but apparently everyone else had not. Liz and Thomas were sitting on the sofa and Claire was kicked back in the recliner. Jack was standing admiring the oceanfront view. I greeted him good morning, glanced out at the waves and turned to ask who would be joining me for church. I went to wash my hair and get ready. Jack came in a few minutes later and said he wanted to show me something. We stepped out on the balcony and he pointed out to the sand. It read, "Bethany, Will you marry me? Jack". He knelt down and presented a ring and asked me again. I looked across the room and there my girls and Thomas sat with big, fat grins on their faces. They were in on it. All three of them, and I was ecstatic! Jack had asked their permission, and they had been scheming for weeks. They had gotten up extra early, and Jack went out and wrote the message with the handle of a shovel while they were his "look outs". I was beside myself with excitement, surprise and joy.

I couldn't think of a better place to celebrate than in God's house. Two hours later Jack and I were worshipping and praising God. My fella was singing with his hand lifted high, and I couldn't have loved him any more than in that moment. We shared communion together and knelt at the altar. As Jack was praying and thanking God for His faithfulness in our lives, His tears fell onto the back of my hand. God had given me the desire of my heart, and then some.

After church we sat outside at the local coffee shop and over chai tea lattes, we called all of our friends and family to tell them the news. It was then that I shared with Jack the lyrics of what would become our song, *A Page is Turned* by Bebo Norman…

A boy and girl each found God, who in the hard knocks of life, was preparing them for each other. God showed them how to dance and gave them each a second chance at love. They became husband and wife. God washed them with grace and let them dance as they promised to hold each other up when the world became unkind as they continued their life together.

The pages of our story would turn, but this time it would be our story, together.

We returned home and started making preparations...preparations for getting married and preparations for sending our little missionary to Honduras. It was not easy to pack her up and send her to a third-world country to live for seven months. Her safety was my biggest concern, and I had to dig down deep for peace in the matter.

It was also time to get back to work. I never looked for another job. I had gone straight to my brother who owned two breakfast and lunch restaurants and told him I wanted to work for him. He grinned and said, "When can you start?" We talked and got a plan together for me to eventually manage one of the locations. I thought, "How stressful can it be? The hardest part of my day will be handling someone's eggs getting scrambled instead of fried."

I started out at the "bottom" taking orders, re-filling coffee cups, and scrubbing toilets. I rolled silverware, put up stock, and counted my tips at the end of the day. Quite humbling. I am great at multi-tasking so this job came naturally, but I felt like a fish out of water. I thought, "What am I doing here? I have three degrees, and I am waiting tables." Oh, I never regretted leaving education, but it was a huge career change to say the least. And, the Lord was teaching me some things. One, I could swallow my pride and be the Bethany He created me to be in my current position. Two, I got over the fear of stranger small talk really quick and could walk right up to customers and break the ice. (I thought to myself, the Lord is going to use this someday, somehow.) Three, He was broadening my territory. I shared His light with a big smile and hearty hello to each guest. Even to my previous school superintendent whose former Teacher of the Year just served him his plate of grits and scrambled eggs.

Our God of Second Chances

*"Delight yourself in the Lord and he will
give you the desires of your heart."*

PSALM 37:4

My house had indeed become my home. I sat on my porch one day watching a red-headed woodpecker jump from tree to tree and heard birds and crickets chiming in. Summer was ending, and so was my time in my home. This was where my daughters grew Godly and strong, rode go-carts and had countless sleepovers. This was where my girlfriends sought Jesus and found Him, ate waffles and shared secrets and dreams. When you give something or someone to the Lord, He gives it back in grand and magnificent ways, covered with His grace and mercy and love. As I breathed in the first hint of fall and watched the last of the lightning bugs, I was reminded of His faithfulness.

In just two months, I would get married and my daughters would help me plan the wedding. I have no words to describe what this meant to me. My greatest desire was for them to be okay, above everything else.

Having your mom get remarried had to be extremely challenging, and they were genuinely happy for me. This put me on cloud nine. They helped me with music, decorating ideas, and went with me to pick out my wedding dress. They kept me grounded and focused.

My girlfriends kept me giddy as we shared in every detail. We celebrated with a bridal photo shoot, a kayaking trip, a bridal shower and a pajama bachelorette party. These two months were the happiest of my life. I was in euphoria and simply could not soak up all that God was blessing me with.

And on Sunday, November 11, 2012, under beautiful fall leaves canopied by a bright blue sky, I became Mrs. Jack Harrison Armstrong. The morning was a sweet bustle of preparations. Lydia brought breakfast, Jenna made the wedding cake, Eden made bows and Patricia took Jack on a prayer walk. We had friends posting signs, heating the church and decorating the reception. There was crispness in the air and boundless joy in our hearts.

As I stood outside the historical country church waiting to walk in, my daughters captivated me. The church was full, the music was playing and there they were, walking ahead of me, leading me to my groom. As I approached, Jack stepped down, walked up to me and escorted me the rest of the way to the altar. With my girls by my side and his sons by his, we exchanged vows and became husband and wife. We had communion together as they played our song. He made me his wife and there was no secret to the Source of our joy. Grace fell like rain and washed us again and gave us a chance to rise above this world where the God of second chances picked us up and let us dance.

Jenna

*"And whatever you do, do it heartily, as to
the Lord and not to men, knowing that from
the Lord you will receive the reward of the
inheritance; for you serve the Lord Christ."*

COLOSSIANS 3:23-24

ack when I ran into Jenna at the singles dance, we quickly exchanged hugs and hellos. It was good to see an old acquaintance in one of my favorite places. I knew her from the education realm and had taught her daughter in school. We became fast friends, sticking together in our singleness while trying to find our "new normals". She was a part of S.A.S. and "Wednesdays at 3" and we often remarked at how parallel our lives were. Here is Jenna's story...

I married at age 18 and was totally devoted to my husband. I spent a great deal of my marriage pleasing him and adapted my whole life around him. I kind of lost myself in the process. We were married 21 years when Neal was diagnosed with leukemia. I became his primary caretaker, and we struggled to get him well. We lived in a daily battle against this disease and with every ounce of our belief we claimed that God would heal him. I covered his hospital room walls with scriptures from family and friends during every admission. Several trips to Emory Hospital in Atlanta and a bone marrow transplant later, we were feeling so hopeful.

We believed in total healing. That came in a way we did not expect. Neal was healed completely, but the Lord took him to heaven to do so.

My life seemed so questionable and in the dark. I had so much hope when Neal got sick, and then when he died I thought, 'What does this mean? Where am I supposed to go now? What am I supposed to do?' I had not prepared for this particular ending. Neal had never given up nor ever confessed that he was going to die. Now what?

I forced myself to go to work because of my kids, but other than that, I stayed in the bed for days and weeks. A dear friend eventually forced me to get up. I had to be a mom for my two kids. I made myself go to work and to church, which was suddenly so very difficult. I couldn't praise God; the songs ripped my soul out, and I did not mean what I was singing. I didn't want anything to do with God. Worship wouldn't come. Tears poured like a river. I often walked out during the service unable to stay due to uncontrollable sobbing. My heart was pained like I had never experienced, my head, so confused. I wanted a word from God. I needed a word from God.

I eventually went to a group grief counsel meeting after seven months, and I saw that there were people still in grief counseling after eight years of their loss. I thought, 'I don't need group counseling. I need God'. On my way home, God brought me to one complete thought - Faith. God did not answer our prayers the way we expected or wanted, but He is still a faithful God. My good and faithful God.

A nurse who cared for Neal and myself during his entire illness became a dear friend to me in my loss because she too had also experienced deep grief from losing her own son. Trish had been given a particular book and in turn, gave the same book to me entitled, "Through a Season of Grief: Devotions for Your Journey from Mourning to Joy" by Bill Dunn and Kathy Leonard, and it was in one of the passages that God spoke to me:

> You may feel as though you have no purpose, that there's nothing left for you to do. This feeling can be particularly strong if your spouse underwent a long illness and you had put all your time and energy into caring for him or her.
>
> Don't get caught up in the fact that you have lost someone but that God has something out there for you and that your life is not over. It may be the beginning of something very special that He has planned for you. It may be something that you would not be able to do if He had kept that one person on earth with you.

You are going to have a new, changed identity. God is calling you for a specific purpose, and you can trust Him to accomplish His purpose in your life.[13]

I had to have the faith and trust that God knew what He was doing in that moment. Why would God take my husband and father of our children away from us? The statement at first made me very angry. If God can do all things, why couldn't He still use us for His purpose without having to take Neal away from his family through cancer? This was a complete turning point for me. I had always lived by the motto that obedience precedes blessing. I had to walk it out before seeing His hand and where he was guiding the rest of my life. My life was about to prove God in all things faith, trust and love. I knew He was all I had at this point. I had to lean on every sense of faith I had. I knew I had to trust Him with my future, my children and my life. I knew that I needed to love Him like I had always loved Him.

I had learned so much while taking care of Neal, and after a year of grief God reminded me of just that. I had voices suddenly resonating "why aren't you a nurse", "you should be nursing". These voices came from the doctors and nurses who saw me caring for Neal during that year-and-a-half battle. God planted the seed, and I now had an interest in going to nursing school. I even visited the hospital unit to get advice from the doctors and nurses to confirm my decision and seek direction. How do I even begin? This gave me a new perspective. I had a desire and motivation to do something that I didn't think possible. I never dreamed I would go to college.

While pursuing this goal, God was also faithful in bringing me some great girlfriends who shared the same experiences. My S.A.S. friends "got me". It wasn't until I met Bethany that I found someone who could relate. It was hard dating at 40 while also raising teenagers. God helped me discover 'me' as a single person, my identity, and that was huge. Discovering Jenna. When I started focusing on school and trying not to be part of a relationship and was okay with that, I found a joy that I did not have before. When it was just me and God, my goals and getting through school, I didn't need anyone else. I didn't need a man to complete me. God was preparing my path, and as long as I was following His direction, He was going to put someone in my path along the way and complete my journey. I think the Lord saw that I was finally grounded in Him and content with being alone. He then brought someone alongside me. Since I wasn't focused on a man, it allowed me to be pursued by a really great guy.

The last eight years have been a "venturing out" of a whole new world and the endless possibilities of God. I didn't know my options, but God has given me so much more. I now have an adventuresome husband who loves sharing life together and introducing new things to me. "God has given me a second chance at love and life" - my new motto. A whole different life than I had before or could ever dream of having. Going back to school. Becoming a nurse.

Having finances to spoil my grandbabies. I never expected a second chance at love. I dreamed of it, but never thought it was possible. I pinch myself thinking, is this true? It seems unreal. I have a husband who loves me and adores me and doesn't hold me down. He gives me options. He lets me love and serve how I like to love and serve. Ned loves me for me and allows me to be the Jenna that God has created. I can seek and discover and love and serve and be me.

Above all, God is a faithful God. He does bring people in and out of our lives to form and shape us for His benefit and purpose, through all seasons of our lives, not just grief. Praise be to God for life and love, friendships and second chances. Thank you Lord, for your unending grace and unconditional love. You truly are a good and faithful God.

~ Jenna

Settling In

*"I will lift up my eyes to the hills; where does
my help come from? My help comes from the
Lord, the maker of heaven and earth."*

PSALM 121:1-2

Moving is hard work. Combining two households into one was even harder. Thank goodness we were still on the mountaintop high of our wedding and Blue Ridge Mountain honeymoon. It would take months to combine, shift, repurpose and donate our earthly belongings. Making our house a home was my goal.

The work was hard emotionally as well. I experienced both tears of joy and sorrow leaving behind my house of 20 years. The living room renovations were extremely symbolic of my new life in Christ. It was the home I had known my entire adult life and the only home my girls knew; leaving just hurt. I was, however, thankful for the timing because my girls were flying the nest for Alabama and Honduras, which were pretty good distractions. But, we would never go home there again.

What took the edge off of leaving that home behind was an incredible provision from the Lord in who He sent to buy it. A precious family whose wife used to come to our house to babysit Claire and Liz after school! She had seen the transformation and understood my deep, spiritual connection with it. In a sense, I was passing the torch of a house that built some spiritually strong women, two of whom were my very own daughters.

I would soon be living in the country, which has so much to offer: sunsets, sunrises, starry skies, and an array of singing birds and buzzing insects. I feel so close to the Lord when in His creation. As Elizabeth Barrett Browning put it, "Earth's crammed with heaven, and every common bush afire with God; But only he who sees, takes off his shoes, the rest sit round it and pluck blackberries, and daub their natural faces unaware."[14]

I didn't want to miss not one bush afire. I used to pine to be able to see the sunset from my own yard. Now I can walk out one door to see the sun set and walk out another door to watch it rise. God has given me more than I could ever ask for. "Taking off my shoes" as Browning puts it, is easy for me to do.

Pastures surround our house at Sandy Acres, and a family member's cows have the liberty to come and go. Up close, cows are beautiful creatures in their own way, and they have a very calming effect. I enjoy hearing a mama cow cry out for her young or watching them all pass by in a single file line as they head to our pond.

A particular cow stole my heart one day when we came across her in the woods. Cows don't live in the woods, but she did. Daisy broke her leg and separated herself from the herd and went to the woods to protect herself, to heal, or to die. A few months later we went back for a picnic and saw her again, hobbling around, eating. She has rejoined the herd now and has a distinguished and painful-looking limp. But she is a survivor. I watch her walk across the pasture headed for the pond with what must seem like miles of territory to cross. But she takes her time and stops to graze along the way. She is always by herself with other cows not too far away.

We are a lot like Daisy. We experience a life-threatening heartbreak or injury and find ourselves alone. We pull away to protect ourselves, to heal, to seek the Lord, or to die. Somewhere in that isolation, in that loneliness, we find strength to heal, to rise up. We find no one there but Him and we cling to Him...hard. We get to a place where we can "come back out" and live again. We struggle, but we manage. Our goals seem miles away, but we take life one step at a time and draw close to Him and graze along the way. We find ourselves among people, but we are set apart. God calls this sanctification. Our suffering draws us so close to Him that even when we are better, we don't want to get all the way back in with the herd. That is a good thing.

It didn't take long for reality to hit. A four-month engagement with euphoric wedding planning, a blissful wedding day and a joyous honeymoon came to an end. I still had my Honey, but it was like coming down from a mountaintop. A depleted savings account needed to be built back up, some health issues clamored for attention, chaotic surroundings and digging out of boxes led to stress, and a demanding work schedule that separated us for weeks took its toll.

"Lord, the sounds I hear are not the same," I prayed one day. "A dog that barks incessantly replaces my choir of tree frogs. I love looking out my kitchen window to watch calves frolic with one another and dance around their mamas. The furniture is the same, but I have some decorating to do to put final touches on our home. The view is incredible. The sky shows the brilliant moon sprinkled with stars that are even brighter in the country. These are the same stars that my husband prayed under. He prayed and you gave him me. But, who am I? I am pondering, scrambling to find me. EVERYTHING about my life is different. Not bad, just very different. I don't cook the same recipes. I don't go to the same job. I don't have Bible study or HomeBase. I don't dress the same or go to church regularly due to work commitments," I said.

Things didn't seem as easy as before. In life, change is inevitable, but trusting God through the transitions is a choice. Some days I chose well, and some days I didn't. Along with change, there is also the "getting used to one another".

For instance, I noticed early on that my Sweet Blessing From Above NEVER used any kind of towel in the kitchen. Not a dishtowel. Not a hand towel. What can I say, my man LOVES PAPER TOWELS. We buy them in bulk because "we don't want to run out". He uses a generous number to wipe his hands and to dry the dishes. He uses them to wipe a spill and to wipe the floor. I remarked one day about how "wasteful" this appears and laid bright, new, colorful kitchen and dishtowels within arm's reach. He never touched them. He continues to use paper towels and, that's okay. I decided to let it go and not let it be something to nag him about. One evening, he left me a note written on, you guessed it, a paper towel. I have a collection of them in my nightstand. As I added this one to the drawer, something dawned on me. If I had continued to harp at him for wasting paper towels, made it an issue, fussed about it, I might have missed all these sweet love notes left on my pillow. *Psalm 19:14 "May the words of my mouth and the meditation of my heart be pleasing in your sight, Lord, my Rock and my Redeemer."*

While I was adjusting to life at Sandy Acres, my youngest blessing was busy changing the world as a missionary in Honduras. Skype was our lifeline. Some days it would reveal a happy, independent teenager who was wise beyond her years, and some days it would show me a homesick, weary traveler ready to come home. Stories of her falling asleep to the sound of gunshots each night, taking taxis driven by locals, or walking to get groceries sent me reeling. This was my first all-out, real exercise in turning sheer worry into prayer. There was absolutely nothing else I could do. I trusted the Lord with her, and He would do great things in and through her. Weeks turned into months, and her time there drew to an end. She shares one of her experiences in the following excerpt:

A Honduran Cub

The smell of tortillas and gasoline filled the air as giggles and small puffy jackets shuffled down the aisle. That rusty school bus had seen more dirt roads than a country song. As I tried my best to fit as many Honduran children onto one leather seat, I saw him. His name was Jonathan, and he barely came up to my waist. I watched as his tight grip clung to his mother's thigh. Little did he know, it was my first day too. I was 18 and had just moved to Honduras to be a missionary and English teacher.

Jonathan crawled onto my lap, and I held him tight as he wept in Spanish all the way to school. That is when I realized I would not only be a teacher to these children, but a mother. A couple of months passed and Jonathan would still cry. I questioned whether it was my class or even the loud, scary school bus. I even asked other Honduran teachers if it could have something to do with the culture that I had not yet learned. After praying over Jonathan and watching him with an extra eye in class, I was still left in the dark.

A few days later, it was just like any other morning. I put on my hunter green school uniform, ate a bagel, and hopped on the bus. As the niños climbed onto the cold, brown seats I peered out of the cracked pane and my heart stopped. I watched Jonathan's mother hit him across his plump cheek and soft brown eye.

He was mine. My kindergartener. My niño. I was a mother who couldn't protect her cub. It was no wonder Jonathan was upset all the time. He was being abused. I walked swiftly off the bus and scooped up my weeping cub. I tried my best to tell the mother bye and to have a good day in my trembling broken Español. She responded as normal and so did Jonathan. He kept crying out to me, "Yo no dice nada." I didn't do anything. I didn't do anything. I shushed him between my neck and shoulder and began to soothe and calm him down. That whole bumpy ride I knew I would have to choose. Either rescue Jonathan by placing him in an orphanage or a family member's home, or discuss the issue with his mamá and hope she would be willing to address the problem. Honduran orphanages are very poor and some of the children do not get fed or clothed simply because the foster parents cannot afford it. Yet, I knew something had to be done. I pondered with our principle for a few days, and we decided to talk to his mother. She admitted she had an issue with her parenting style and wanted better for Jonathan and herself.

Over the next few months she attended counseling classes and I continued to keep my eye on my adopted cub. The school year came to a close and so did my time in Honduras. I have to hope that I made a difference by standing up for Jonathan that day. And, I have to pray that while I am here in the United States that God is watching over a sweet, little Honduran boy who will live in my heart forever.

~Liz

And while she was in Honduras packing her bags to come home, my heart busted with this tribute to my missionary....

I can see you swaying with each stop of the bus to brace yourself against the five students who share your seat.
I can see the back of their heads as they bobble up and down the dirt roads of a poor city.
I can hear them calling out to you, "Teacher, teacher!" as the soccer ball whizzes by.
I can hear your young neighbors beckoning you to come out and play or hand them something to eat.
I see their smiles as they enter your classroom, a safe haven from poverty and pain.
I see you bending over, tying 30 pair of wet, dirty shoelaces.
They know more English. You know more Spanish.
Way down where you cannot see, their hearts are forever marked by the love of Jesus carried by your words, your smile, your touch.
They will never be the same. Neither will you.
You went to make a difference.
You went to be "His" favorite.
Welcome Home, Liz!

Matthew 25:21 states, "His master replied, 'Well done, good and faithful servant! You have been faithful with a few things; I will put you in charge of many things. Come and share your master's happiness!'"

Part 5

Identity Crisis

Who Am I?

"See, I have engraved you on the palm of my hands; your walls are ever before me."

ISAIAH 49:16

For reasons I cannot fully explain, I experienced separation anxiety from my husband, almost to the point of being unhealthy. Almost. If he was scheduled to be at home, and I had to go to work, I would be so anxious to the point I was unsettled until I returned home. This drove me to an incessant pursuit of getting our work schedules to match. We would do everything together. He would ask me to go with him to get his hair cut or to his doctor's appointments, and I willingly obliged. I noticed that I wasn't getting much done this way, but it didn't matter. My day and my world revolved around Jack. I think we were just so much in love and even though God understood that, He didn't want that idol to continue.

Work would call him away for weeks at a time. We would stand in the driveway and cry as we said our goodbyes. It was unnatural to be apart as husband and wife. I don't know how service members and their families do it. I was lonely and felt myself drifting into depression. It wasn't just being away from my husband, but an underlying issue of not knowing who I was anymore. So much had changed in the last few years. Life is all about change, but I had experienced many huge changes simultaneously.

An unexpected divorce of a 22-year-long marriage, retiring from the teaching profession after 21 years, both of my daughters flying the nest, moving from the house that was a home for 20 years, marrying again and taking a new job in my family's business all led to experiencing a major identity crisis. I no longer knew who I was. I wasn't the wife, the teacher or the mom I used to be; the house that I remodeled to make mine, no longer was. It…was…paralyzing. This led to a serious lack of motivation and depression. I was miserable and couldn't get anything done. I had no priority in my life. Oh, I went to work and took care of the home, but that was about it. I felt lost. I was simply existing. The tail was definitely wagging the dog, and I needed to get a handle on my priorities, or lack there of.

In the six months that I experienced this paralyzing identity crisis, I never questioned where God was. I knew He was with me and that I belonged to Him, I just didn't feel Him close. I was in a desert. There was a direct correlation between the time I put into seeking Him and how close I felt His presence. I needed to make some changes and do what I knew to do. Get in His Word. Study. Be with Him in the mornings. This excerpt speaks of the importance of doing this very thing:

The Drawing Room

A man named Robert Munger tells how he showed Christ around the house of his heart, inviting him to "settle down there and be perfectly at home," welcoming him room by room.

Together they visited the library of his mind - a very small room with very thick walls. They peered into the dining room of his appetites and desires. They spent a little time in the workshop where his talents and skills were kept, and the rumpus room of "certain associations and friendships, activities and amusements." They even poked their heads into the hall closet filled with dead, rotting things he managed to hoard. The drawing room was significantly special...

We walked next into the drawing room. This room was rather intimate and comfortable. I liked it. It had a fireplace, overstuffed chairs, a bookcase, sofa, and a quiet atmosphere.

Christ also seemed pleased with it. He said, "This is indeed a delightful room. Let us come here often. It is secluded and quiet and we can have fellowship together."

Well, naturally, as a young Christian I was thrilled. I could not think of anything I would rather do than have a few minutes apart with Christ in intimate comradeship.

Jesus promised, "I will be here every morning early. Meet with Me here and we will start the day together." So, morning after morning, I would come downstairs to the drawing room and He would take a book of the Bible....open it and then we would read together. He would tell me of its riches and unfold me its truths... They were wonderful hours together. In fact, we called the drawing room the "withdrawing room." It was a period when we had our quiet time together.

But little by little, under the pressure of many responsibilities, this time began to be shortened.... I began to miss a day now and then.... I would miss it two days in a row and often more.

I remember one morning when I was in a hurry.... As I passed the drawing room, the door was ajar. Looking in I saw a fire in the fireplace and the Lord sitting there.… "Blessed Master, forgive me. Have You been here all these mornings?"

"Yes," He said, "I told you I would be here every morning to meet with you." Then I was even more ashamed. He had been faithful in spite of my faithlessness. I asked His forgiveness and He readily forgave me.….

He said, "The trouble with you is this: You have been thinking of the quiet time, of the Bible study and prayer time, as a factor in your own spiritual progress, but you have forgotten that this hour means something to Me also."[15]

What an amazing thought---that Christ wants to spend quality time with me. That He looks forward to our time together and misses me when I don't show up. I surrendered my time to Him and became intentional about seeking Him each morning. He was counting on it, I needed it, and so did the people in my life. They were depending on me. After all, we had another wedding to plan!

John came to our house in his dress blues and asked for Claire's hand in marriage. He sat next to me on the couch and told me he loved her and that he wanted to spend the rest of his life with her. Tacked on to this marriage proposal would be a trip to Japan, a trip that would last three years. They would be stationed there as he pursued his career in the Army. They would have no one there but each other, and had plans to see the world.

He proposed on the night of my parent's 50th wedding anniversary celebration and they set the wedding date for forty-two days later. If anyone could pull off a complete wedding with nothing left out, it was my very efficient and organized first-born. The month was a whirlwind of planning and preparation, and it all fell into place. On February 1, 2014, my daughter became Mrs. John Robert Winston. Early that morning, traces of snow were on the ground as I made my way to the cabins where the wedding party spent the night. I crept into the room where my soon-to-be daughter bride was sleeping next to her sister/Maid of Honor. It was so sweet to wake her up on her wedding day. John and Claire exchanged "I dos" in grand military splendor, complete with the cutting of the wedding cake with his military sabre. They honeymooned in Asheville, NC and would live in North Carolina for a few months before moving to Japan.

Can we talk about that a second? Japan. Japan is 6,200 miles away on the other side of the world. It is not accessible by highway. Japan is on a 13-hour time difference. She knows NO ONE in Japan. There was nothing that could have ever prepared me for this. I knew Claire would grow up and move away one day, but I never imagined it would be clear across the world. I could not bear the thought of not seeing her and not being able to do things together. I fretted and I cried. I cried and I worried. I just couldn't help it.

Part of the depression that I vacillated in and out of was due to the coming and going of the three people closest to me. Coming was the great part; the going, not so much. My husband's work schedule had him away for a week at a time, and as I mentioned, it was unnatural. What *was* natural but still painful, were my daughters coming home to visit or to stay for a while and then leaving again. The revolving door on my house had my heart doing somersaults.

That surrender to know God on a much deeper level and to seek Him each morning through the study of his Word was paying off. It was my lifeline as I attempted to handle the thought of my daughter living so far away from me. She wouldn't be just flying the nest; she would be flying very far away.

God was faithful in giving me incredible peace. He helped me realize that Japan is no further from *Him* than Alabama or North Carolina or, Madison, GA. Knowing that she and her husband would be finding their way through a new culture, a new language, new friends and a new home together was heartwarming. They would look back on this time one day and relish the memories, adventures and time of bonding as newlyweds. I'm sure I will be long gone...having left my own nest... for Home.

> *"Who am I, O Sovereign Lord, and what is my family, that you have brought me this far? And as if this were not enough in your sight, O Sovereign Lord, you have also spoken about the future of the house of your servant. And now, Lord God, keep forever the promise you have made concerning your servant and his house. Do as you promised, so that your name will be great forever. Now be pleased to bless the house of your servant, that it may continue forever in your sight; for you, O Sovereign Lord, have spoken, and with your blessing the house of your servant will be blessed forever."*
> 1 SAM 7:18, 25-29

Heartstring Tug of War

"He has made everything beautiful in its time. He has also set eternity in the human heart; yet no one can fathom what God has done from beginning to end."

ECCLESIASTES 3:11

*B*eing the mother of young twenty-somethings is a delicate and precarious time for mamas. We have to learn how to "be there" but be silent; how to be available, but be "hands off"; how to know when to let them do it, make decisions, trust them, and trust God. We have to recognize that our role has changed, and that we are not responsible for them anymore, whether they are single or married. We have to let them go and hold on tight to them through prayer because sometimes, that's all we can do.

I was savoring my last few days with Claire before she and John left for Japan, and I was hanging on to every tiny detail...how we were elbow to elbow putting on mascara, how she hung her robe on the back of the bathroom door, how she peered into the bedroom at him as he was sleeping and said, "Isn't he so cute?" How she shuffled across the room after answering the door with a response of, "I don't know. Let me go ask my husband." "She has a HUSBAND," I thought to myself.

Additionally, I had to watch Liz apprehensively "tango with her landlord" over many issues she was having with the house she rented at college. I was a listening ear and offered suggestions, but she did not want me to step in for fear that she may suffer the consequences later. It bothered me that she had to deal with this, but I knew that doing so would only make her stronger.

Also, she had the honor and privilege of being a co-leader for the Women of Wesley in Milledgeville the following fall. She created activities and ran her ideas by me, which left me awestruck, amazed, and secretly wanting to be a Wesley girl. This would be an overwhelming responsibility for her, and it would require much time and planning on her part, in addition to her full class load. I planned to be sitting on "go" when she needed me, but I knew that this was something that only she could really do.

I continued to dust my empty nest while keeping my ear to the wind, listening for the call of "Mama..."

"There is a time for everything, and a season for every activity under heaven." ECCLESIASTES 3:1

Japan Bound

*"Create in me a clean heart, O God, and renew
a right spirit within me. Cast me not away from
your presence, and take not your Holy Spirit
from me. Restore to me the joy of your salvation
and grant me a willing spirit to sustain me."*

PSALM 51:10-12

The time came for Claire and John to fly to Japan. Both families met in Charleston, SC to see them off at the airport. Of all mornings, Claire woke up with a full-blown sinus infection, which would not be good on a 15-hour flight. We started the morning at the local prompt care and got loaded up with medications. Needless to say, this mama was even more unsettled about her leaving. You know how we are when our kids are sick.

Our "party" of ten later filled the hotel shuttle and headed to the airport. Every step we took through the check in process got heavier and heavier for me as I knew they would take me one step closer to saying goodbye. To my delight, John managed to get the whole group gate passes so that we could sit with them until they boarded. This bought me two more hours with my first-born blessing. We ordered lunch, but I couldn't swallow past the lump in my throat. The newlywed adventurers giggled and posed for pictures with their boarding passes marked "Japan". They were chipper and smiled, but I could sense a little anxiety in Claire. I sat as close to her as I could.

Their flight was called to board, and I had to say goodbye. It was one of the hardest things I have ever had to do. I tried hard not to make a spectacle of myself and did well considering the circumstances. It felt so heavy saying goodbye with a magnetic pull/push in both directions. I cried the whole way out of the airport. Jack, Liz, Thomas and I walked outside and around the building to the tarmac. We watched their plane take off into the sunset bound for Asia where they would begin their life together. Alone. How could something be so painful and beautiful at the same time?

Liz and I walked side by side with our arms on each other's shoulders all the way to the car. It would just be the two of us. Our close mother-daughter-sister bond was now altered. I balled and worried, and Liz listened and encouraged. Jack and Thomas followed behind us in another vehicle. On the three-hour drive home, my rock-solid, wise-beyond-her-years co-pilot helped this mama settle as best she could. I was a mess for weeks. I would be fine one minute, and then out of the blue without warning came a watershed of tears.

I thought about how a mama travels whatever road necessary to get to her offspring. I have traveled to Athens to see Claire and then to Birmingham and Fayetteville. It felt good knowing the roads that would take me to her. I did the same thing and followed the roads that led me to Liz in Milledgeville. I came to realize that the Lord used these opportunities to prepare me for such a long-distance separation from them both. Every new city that they called their home was a step that the Lord used to gird me. God was faithful in the heartbreaking time of empty nesting. He wastes nothing.

One evening I was lying under a canopy of stars smelling the fresh cut grass and could hear a mama cow calling for her calf. If the calf gets too far away, the mama will call, and the calf will answer. This lasts for about four months, and then the calf is old enough to wander and doesn't have to be watched closely. I think this is where Claire and I are. A shepherd has a distinct call for his sheep. He may use the same word as another shepherd when gathering his flock after they have mingled with another. However, the sheep only respond to the voice of their shepherd, his tone. They know his voice distinctly from all others. I prayed that Claire was listening for her Shepherd's voice. I felt like I passed the torch, and that the Lord was fully in charge of the one who belonged to Him all along.

Counting Blessings

*"Enter his gates with thanksgiving and his courts
with praise; give thanks to him and praise his name.
For the Lord is good and his love endures forever; his
faithfulness continues through all generations."*

PSALM 100:4

Though I don't like to admit it, I fell into a desert season with the Lord. My passion was gone even though I was seeking? I pose this as a question because I *was* seeking. Lydia and I both kept a Bible study before us, but we struggled in feeling distant from God despite that fact. This went on for months and we met, prayed and talked about it. Was it the proverbial midlife crisis? Empty nesting, still? Our physical bodies wearing down? Were we just worn out from life? We posed these questions to each other and to the Lord. From week to week, we did what we knew to do...prayed, studied, encouraged one another and counted our blessings.

We wanted the passion back and to feel the fire, the excitement and Jesus-giddiness. The Lord knew this. God always knows our hearts. He showed me that my heart was divided. I had other people and things in there with Him, and he wanted sole custody of my heart! In studying *David- Seeking a Heart Like His* by Beth Moore, I learned that if my heart is divided it puts my life in jeopardy.

> Only God can be totally trusted with our hearts. He doesn't demand our complete devotion to feed His ego but to provide for our safety. God uses an undivided heart to keep us out of trouble. David learned the price of a divided heart the hard way. He lived with the repercussions for the rest of his life.[16]

For me it was the monotonous, frustrating, physically demanding job at the restaurant, anxiety about money, worrying about what others thought, and wanting what was best for my family's business that all seemed to be pushing God into a corner of my heart. *I Chronicles 22:19 says, "Now devote your heart and soul to seeking the Lord your God."* David told Solomon and Israel's leaders to fasten their hearts to seeking the Lord. I desired to do the same. I wanted to honor God, to be willing and to be obedient.

God showed me that my current circumstances and environment were keeping me from using my talents and gifts to do what He called me to do. Ephesians 2:10 states, " *For we are God's handiwork, created in Christ Jesus to do good works, which God prepared in advance for us to do."* And *2 Timothy 3:16 says, "All Scripture is God-breathed and is useful for teaching, rebuking, correcting and training in righteousness, so that the servant of God may be thoroughly equipped for every good work."*

I am flooding you with all of these Scriptures because they spoke to me and gave me direction. That's what God's Word will do! This is how He speaks directly to us and to our situations.

"Now begin the work, and the Lord be with you." 1 Chronicles 22:16

I decided to surrender my job and meager income to make myself available to write, to use my experiences and wisdom so that others may know Him. What story did I have to tell? He gave me a new life, He became my first love again, He filled me with His power, He showed Himself faithful in my finances, and He brought me out of my comfort zone to show me who I was in Him. His was the story worth telling.

So, we have come full circle. This is where the story began, but not quite where it ends…

I spent several months clearing my head, praying for direction and transitioning out of work responsibilities. I began to write and sought Him for direction on how to go about it. With trust and faith that God had a plan, I pursued His calling on my life and began to pen His story for you. Do you know what he did as a result? He blessed me. Abundantly. With a part-time teaching position two days a week that was a great supplement to our income and gave me five days a week to work on writing. I was not even considering a job, much less looking. All of the reasons that I left education would not be an issue in this new position. It was truly a teacher's dream job. Jobs like this just didn't exist, or at least I didn't think they did.

Cupid was at it again as a tutoring relationship turned into full-blown love between Liz and Thomas. They supported each other through a seven-month mission trip to Honduras and being apart at college. Thomas was ready to make it official, and we planned and schemed for months to help him. On a crisp, fall afternoon in the middle of a pecan orchard, he got on his knee and asked Liz to marry him. Jack and I were discreetly taking pictures and came out of hiding on cue. We cheered and hugged and took more pictures. Then, to Liz's astonishment, her big sister popped out and surprised her. All the way from Japan! She and John flew home to be a part of their special day. The sheer sister love, leap of joy, uncontrollable sobs and tear-drenched hair was a once in a lifetime memory. Liz told us that the only thing that she truly wanted to make her proposal special one day was for Claire to be able to be there for it, and she had resolved herself to the fact that it just wasn't going to happen because Claire lived out of the country. Claire told Liz that she wouldn't have missed it for the world.

Thomas and Liz were scheduled to graduate in May so a wedding date was set for June. That gave us eight months to plan the wedding.

On a weekend trip home to have one of her wedding dress fittings, I had a prior commitment. I asked Liz what her dinner plans were, and she said she thought she would ask Jack if he wanted to go to Panera Bread. I got home before they did. When they walked in the door, Jack was carrying roses for me, she was carrying mixed flowers that he bought her, and they had just come back from visiting my parents where Jack took my mama flowers and my daddy ice cream. Just picture that scene with me. My heart was overflowing. I thought back to the struggle I had in wanting my girls to be okay with my new relationship. Now I was seeing God's faithfulness in this area, and it was more than I could have imagined.

The wedding was dreamy. Perfect in every way. They honeymooned in Charleston, SC and settled down in Jacksonville, FL where Thomas would attend graduate school. They knew no one. What was it about my youngins that made them do this? I raised them to be independent, but couldn't they do it a little closer to home? I was proud of all of them. It was just hard. I missed grabbing lunch, shopping, or sitting to chat. I knew the positive side to this would be that they would only have each other, and it would solidify their foundation as newly married couples.

To say that the enemy was prowling was an understatement. He was using every opportunity to pull me down into a lonely depression even though I was active, had handfuls of girlfriends and a sweet, humble husband. I really struggled being separated from my two daughters.

They say divorce is hard because two have become one and then you have the tearing apart of that. As a mother, conceiving, giving birth and raising a child starts off as one from the beginning. Then they leave. It is a ripping apart like nothing else on earth, and you are never quite the same. There are moms who have lost children to death, those whose kids have gone wayward, those who have them living just around the corner, and those that fall everywhere else in between. It is painfully natural. It is bitter-sweet. It is a paralyzing freedom.

There were days I didn't move off of the couch, days I merely went through the motions and days I felt lost. There were also days I embraced my extra me-time, days I accomplished much, and days I was able to spend time with other people I love.

I got a puppy, led continuous Bible studies and took a major leadership role in ministry with Walk to Emmaus. The "up days" stretched into "up weeks" and then "up months" with the occasional pining in my heart to just be in the presence of my daughters. Texts, phone calls and Skype sessions had to be enough. Sometimes they were. When they weren't, I just used all that "missing energy" to pray for them, and to count my blessings. I had more than any one person deserved.

All Creatures Great and Small

"How great is your goodness, which you have stored up for those who fear you, which you bestow in the sight of men on those who take refuge in you."

PSALM 31:19

My "empty nesting" puppy is full-grown now and is the dog I have always wanted. Rusty follows me from room to room and lies at my feet. He is great company when I'm alone and my constant companion. I remember the day I got him, sort of on a whim, and how I felt guilty for not praying about such a big decision beforehand. God knew exactly what I needed, even when I did not, or bothered to ask Him about first. Rusty has been an incredible blessing. *In Every Season* is all about God's continued faithfulness through every season of our lives. He is always working in advance of our needs, and He wants us to trust Him in the meantime.

I hope that you have also seen how God brings good out of what satan means for harm. I'll leave you with one final example of these two characteristics of our Lord.

One afternoon, I received a call from Liz in Jacksonville, FL. She was home alone working in her office at four in the afternoon and got up to investigate a noise. She turned the corner and standing in her den was a man who had cut the porch window screen and jimmied the sliding glass door to get inside. She screamed and ran out the front door. He bolted out of the same window he had cut to climb in. Thankfully he was there for valuables and assumed no one was home.

The police began investigating, Thomas rushed to her side, and I drove to spend a few days with her. Leaving her to come home was very difficult, but we knew I would have to eventually. She had been robbed of her sense of security and did not feel safe in her own home. Who could? We put some safety measures in place, but every little noise sent her reeling. She needed something more, and the puppy search began.

There was nothing available in Jacksonville that she was interested in adopting so she broadened her search to the Madison, GA area. She sent me a couple of pictures and off to animal services I went for the preliminary screening. The puppy I went to see was way too small. I showed the lady a picture of another puppy that Liz sent me. This one looked promising, but I was told it was picked up as a stray and could not be viewed until tomorrow, the day it would either be put up for adoption or euthanized. I went and asked Archer, the person in charge, if it was available. He took me to see it and the mixed dachshund was EXACTLY what Liz was looking for! Archer said if we wanted him, we could have him. Liz drove five hours to Madison the next day and adopted him. She told me that when she was doing her search, she had "accidentally" clicked on lost dogs where she saw Cooper's picture instead of the dogs available for adoption.

I'm not sure who rescued whom. I think both. As I watched her leave my driveway with him in her front seat, tears filled my eyes. God had given my girl exactly what she needed.

Here at home, we have added 26 cows and a herd bull to Sandy Acres, which has catapulted us into full-time beef cattle farmers. It will be extra retirement income and also enable us to be good stewards of the land with which the Lord has blessed us. I have been surprised at how much I love farm life. I enjoy getting dirt under my fingernails and sweating to make things happen. I have learned how to mend fences, drive the tractor, front-end loader and all, and carry sixty pounds of feed like a beast.

The cows are eating for two now, so in a few months, we will have a pasture full of calves. Three donkeys are here waiting their arrival; their job is to ward off coyotes that live in the woods.

My days begin with watching the sun come up over the pasture, and they end with watching it set as we ride around the property checking the fence line. Each day, we pass the white oak tree that we planted in the very spot where we shared coffee ice cream at midnight on our first date. We call it the "moon bow tree". I have never felt physically closer to the Lord than I do at Sandy Acres. His very creation draws me near.

What draws you near to Him? We all have a unique and different story. Without Jesus, we really don't have one at all. If you feel like something is missing from your life, it is most likely a relationship with Him. All you have to do is invite Him into your heart and accept Him as your Lord and Savior. Acknowledge your sins before Him, no matter what they are, and accept His forgiveness. Then, be sure to share your decision with someone who can guide you on your new path forward with the Lord.

As I share the story I never thought I had or could share, I am still in awe of the faithfulness and miracles of God. He keeps adding to my story, just as He does yours. I smile when I think about His incredible timing and orchestration of even the smallest details of my life. I am also reeling at His mighty work in me, and how much He loves me, no matter what. I'm amazed at how He looks at me as holy because He sees Jesus in me. I am grateful that He set this girl free!

God has given you a story, too. I pray that you will allow Him to write on the pages of your heart and bless you, too, with unspeakable peace and joy.

To God be the glory, for great things He has done.

To the Reader

What is your story? The following blank pages are for you to write down how God has been faithful in your life. Then, pass the book along to someone you think will be encouraged by all of our stories, and then they can do the same. How God has been faithful in our lives is a story worth telling.

I would love to hear from you and have an opportunity to pray for you. Feel free to contact me at ineveryseason12@gmail.com.

Abundant blessings and favor to you, dear friend!

Bethany

Your Story

Your Story

Your Story

Your Story

Your Story

Your Story

Your Story

Your Story

Notes

Scriptures

The Holy Bible, New International Version, (Grand Rapids, Michigan: Zondervan, 1984)

"Never Say Never"

1. Joanna Weaver, *Having a Mary Spirit*, (Colorado Springs, Colorado: Waterbrook Press, 2006), 247.

"I'll Do Anything"

2. Joanna Weaver, *Having a Mary Heart in a Martha World*, (Colorado Springs, Colorado: Waterbrook Press, 2002), 205.

"HomeBase"

3. Arthur Christopher Bacon, quoted in Mrs. Charles E. Cowman, *Streams in the Desert in Zondevan Treasures: Streams in the Desert and Springs in the Valley* (Grand Rapids: Zondervan, 1996), 48-49.

"Expect the Unexpected"

4. Oswald Chambers, *The Golden Book of Oswald Chambers: My Utmost for His Highest,* Christian Library Edition (Westwood, NJ: Barbour, 1963), May 24.

"Tearing Away"

5. Ann Spangler, *Praying the Names of God,* (Grand Rapids, Michigan: Zondervan, 2004), 72.

"The Inevitable"

6. Ann Spangler, *Praying the Names of God,* (Grand Rapids, Michigan: Zondervan, 2004), 68.

7. Joanna Weaver, *Having a Mary Spirit,* (Colorado Springs, Colorado: Waterbrook Press, 2006), 103.

"Trading Ashes for Beauty"

8. Beth Moore, *Esther: It's Tough Being a Woman,* (Nashville, TN: Lifeway Press, 2009), 104.

9. Nicholas Sparks, *Three Weeks with My Brother,* (New York, NY: Grand Central Publishing, 2006), 263.

"First Place"

10. John and Stasi Eldredge, *Captivating,* (Nashville, TN: Thomas Nelson, 2005), 113.

11. Eldredge, *Captivating,* 115.

12. Henry and Richard Blackaby, *Experiencing God,* (Nashville, TN: Lifeway Press, 2009), 116.

"Jenna"

13. Patricia in Bill Dunn and Kathy Leonard,*"Through a Season of Grief: Devotions for Your Journey from Mourning to Joy,* (Nashville, TN: Nelson Books, 2004), 134.

"Settling In"

14. Elizabeth Barrett Browning, http://www.seeingcreation.com/tag/elizabeth-barrett-browning/, accessed August 4, 2016.

"Who Am I?"

15. Robert Boyd Munger, *My Heart Christ's Home*, (London, England: Inter-Varsity Press, March 20, 1986), pamphlet.

"Counting Blessings"

16. Beth Moore, *David: Seeking a Heart Like His*, (Nashville, TN: Lifeway Press, 2012), 228.

Made in the USA
Columbia, SC
15 May 2021